Journey through the Word

Exploring Biblical Themes

James E. Davison
and
Sara Covin Juengst

Westminster John Knox Press
LOUISVILLE • LONDON

© 2003 James E. Davison and Sara Covin Juengst

Scripture quotations, unless otherwise indicated, are from the New Revised Standard Version of the Bible, copyright © 1989 by the Division of Christian Education of the National Council of the Churches of Christ in the U.S.A., and used by permission.

Scripture quotations marked RSV are from the Revised Standard Version of the Bible, copyright © 1946, 1952, 1971, and 1973 by the Division of Christian Education of the National Council of the Churches of Christ in the U.S.A., and are used by permission.

Book design by Sharon Adams
Cover design by Pam Poll Graphic Design
Cover art: "Woman Crossing Bridge" © Nicholas Wilton/SIS

First edition
Published by Westminster John Knox Press
Louisville, Kentucky

This book is printed on acid-free paper that meets the American National Standards Institute Z39.48 standard. ⊗

PRINTED IN THE UNITED STATES OF AMERICA

03 04 05 06 07 08 09 10 11 12 — 10 9 8 7 6 5 4 3 2 1

Library of Congress Cataloging-in-Publication Data is on file at the Library of Congress, Washington, D.C.

ISBN 0-664-22616-7

With thanks to our spouses and friends,
Dan Juengst and Reeny Davison,
for their unwavering support and care,
and for sharing their lives with us.

Contents

Preface

This book had its inception at a Bible Study Skills Retreat at the Montreat Conference Center in Montreat, North Carolina in the summer of 1999. The goal of that retreat was "to deepen the understanding and interpretation not only of individual themes but also of the Scriptures as a whole." That is also our goal for this text. The title has a double meaning. We believe that it is only "through the Word" itself that we can begin to understand the richness of the themes presented in this study, many of which have been corrupted by secular nuances. We believe also that by journeying "through the Word" in a chronological fashion, we can discern the way in which these themes build on one another, creating a substantial scaffolding for the basic structure of our faith.

This study has been designed as an eight-week Bible study for adults. Each session is planned for one hour. It is our hope that those who engage in this study will do so with intentionality and commitment. The detailed lesson plans for each chapter include a variety of interactive teaching methods, designed to help the participants relate the themes to their own lives. The true value of this study will be available only if participants are willing to do the assigned Scripture readings and exercises. It is not enough that you hear someone talk about the Bible; it is crucial that you read it yourself!

SARA COVIN JUENGST
JAMES E. DAVISON

Chapter 1

Creation

The first chapter of the book of Genesis tells us about the origins of the universe. At the beginning there was God. At God's command, the entire universe came into being. Out of nothing, heavens and earth were shaped into an immense, marvelous world inhabited by star clusters and galaxies, by planets and comets, by microscopic seeds and grains of sand. Then, Genesis 1 proclaims, created at the end of the process stands a being that bears God's own likeness. Human beings, men and women, are the crown of this creation. They are intended to live in this world as responsible caretakers, and at the same time this world is meant for their enjoyment.

At one time or another, you may have heard the remarkable sermon on creation by the great African American preacher James Weldon Johnson, who lived in the first half of the twentieth century. The sermon begins as God looks out on the vast emptiness of space and experiences a kind of lonesomeness and isolation. After some reflection God says simply, "I'm lonely." Then God decides to create a world. The remainder of the sermon follows the story of creation in Genesis 1, describing in picturesque and unforgettable language how the majestic God of the universe fashions—with vision, insight, and great tenderness—the world in which we find ourselves.

The climax comes when God decides to form human beings. Johnson portrays God, the Almighty One who has made earth and sun and stars, kneeling down at a riverbank, "like a mammy bending over her baby." God shapes a lump of clay into human form, breathes God's breath into it, and humans come into being.[1] Johnson's sermon portrays in a warm and poetic way what a personal and loving act God's creation of the universe must have been. Doesn't that image of God kneeling over the first human being "like a mammy bending over

1

her baby" bring the gentle and tender heart of the Lord to life in an unforgettable way?

Creation in the Book of Genesis

Creation is arguably the central theme in the Scriptures. In the first place, it is the precondition for other themes we will consider in this book. After all, without creation, we couldn't talk about any other themes at all. In the second place, the theme of creation is also a reminder that our origins go back to a stunning divine desire. They go back to a decision by God. It is a free, unfettered decision to make a world, to create a universe. Johnson's sermon puts this thought poetically in the words "I'm lonely . . . I'll make me a world." In more theological terminology, this theme reminds us that God is eternal and exists forever. In contrast, the world and all that is in it, including us, has a beginning, or a point of origin. Not only does it have a beginning, but the world may also have an end.

If you stop to think about it, we see signs of that every day. A lovely flower blossoms, but then it fades away. Lovely plants and shrubs may last for years, and giant sequoias may live for centuries, but eventually they are all felled by wind or fire, by disease, or simply by old age. "Nothing lasts forever," we say, but don't we somehow hope that won't apply to us? Even the stars have births and deaths, and so our own planet is destined eventually to pass away. Our world and all that is in it is dependent on God's goodness and favor to continue in existence. Only the eternal God is everlasting.

We can get at this theme of creation by looking closely at the first chapter of Genesis. As you read through the chapter, notice how each day is summarized with the phrase "and there was evening and there was morning." Day 1 can serve as an example:

> Then God said, "Let there be light"; and there was light. And God saw that the light was good; and God separated the light from the darkness. God called the light Day, and the darkness he called Night. And there was evening and there was morning, the first day. (Gen. 1:3–5)[2]

You may be aware of the reason for this odd-sounding phrase. For the ancient Hebrews, and for Jewish people today, "day" begins at nightfall. Thus, the Sabbath, which we usually think of as Saturday, begins on Friday evening.

This refrain of "evening and morning" suggests already that there is an orderliness to God's creation of heaven and earth. This orderliness also comes to the fore in terms of what is created on individual days. In particular, notice what happens on each of the first three days. If you compare that to what occurs on days 4 through 6, you will notice a similar movement in the two sets of three days.

You may be aware that certain numbers were considered sacred among peoples of the ancient world. The number three was one such number. Seven was another. Three could imply the Divine, and it suggested completion. Thus this text implies that in each set of three days, God created something complete and well rounded. Two sets of three—with each set integrated with the other—give us the picture of an orderly, structured creation. On top of that, following the divine creation, we read that "God rests." This, of course, adds a seventh day to the whole. Seven is another number that implies completion or perfection. This final day, then, offers another hint of the complete, orderly manner in which this creation came into being.

Now, note that, for the surrounding Mesopotamian culture, the conception of this world and the assumptions of its origin were considerably different. By and large, people felt that the world was chaotic: there seemed to be neither rhyme nor reason to what occurred. What was, simply was. The gods had accomplished no divine plan that could keep the various pieces of earthly life working in some sort of sensible, proper manner. Chaos was the name of the game. In contrast, the picture in Genesis 1 of the days of creation proclaims pointedly that God is in control of things both as they are made and after they have come into being. God creates in a sensible, coherent, orderly manner.

There is much more in these verses, of course, but let's consider just one further, highly significant detail. Have you pondered the fact that the sun, moon, and stars appear on the fourth day? Contrary to our scientific understanding that the sun and other stars are the *cause* of light, the picture here is just the reverse. The Light presents itself first, and stars and the sun serve only as signs, or tokens, of that light. That may seem odd, until you remember that this description is meant to challenge the prevailing religious beliefs of the time. In stark contrast to the Mesopotamian and other cultures of the day, the writer is making a highly important point here: the sun, the moon, and other natural phenomena are not divine. They are not divinities to be worshiped, only lovely parts of the creation of Almighty God. Others may wish to worship them, but such religious commitments are wrong-headed. Far from being gods, the sun and the moon were not even created until the fourth day.

Genesis 1, in other words, is a theological statement about who God is and what God's world is like. You might call it a statement of faith. As it did in early times, this chapter continues in the present to stand in sharp contrast to other, competing visions of this world. For example, Eastern religions tend to view the physical world as inferior to the soul, or inner reality. The physical world is more likely to be a hindrance than a help in cultivating our deepest selves. Thus we are encouraged to minimize the influence of the world on our lives. The biblical vision, to the contrary, affirms the whole of creation, and it encourages us to rejoice in the world of the senses as well as in the world of the spirit. We will see this in greater detail as we move through this chapter.

In a different direction, our modern and sometimes atheistic culture tends to see this world as accidental. It is simply the result of random events and processes. Ultimately, the world is an impersonal, cold universe. The Scriptures, however, do not see the world as accidental or cold but as a valuable, orderly, warm place. This cannot be affirmed more strongly than in God's final verdict in Genesis 1, as we see the Lord of heaven and earth standing back and surveying all that has been made: "Behold, it was very good" (Gen. 1:31 KJV).

The Beauty of Creation

A well-known old hymn begins with the words "For the beauty of the earth."[3] Have you ever been awestruck by the beauty of the earth? Is there a particular kind of terrain, a special kind of flower, or a specific kind of animal that calls to mind for you the thought that God's world is beautiful? The Israelites were keen observers of nature, and they, too, found this earth—and the heavens—to be a place of awe and splendor.

Psalm 104 is an example of this. As you read the psalm, notice what a detailed picture emerges of "the beauty of the earth." After extolling the majesty of the Creator God, who is "wrapped in light as with a garment" (104:2), the psalmist praises the magnificence of this created world, with its solid foundations and endless waters, its grassy plains and imposing mountains. Everywhere the psalmist looks, he observes places prepared for living things of all sorts: birds nesting in the cedars of Lebanon, goats climbing on high cliffs, lions roaring in the night, and creatures swimming in the sea while ships sail upon it. This world is orderly, says the psalmist. It is charming. God has created everything carefully and tenderly.

This same delight surfaces in the great theologian of Geneva, John Calvin. In his *Institutes of the Christian Religion*, Calvin writes that

> wherever you cast your eyes, there is no spot in the universe wherein you cannot discern at least some sparks of [God's] glory. You cannot in one glance survey this most vast and beautiful system of the universe, in its wide

expanse, without being completely overwhelmed by the boundless force of its brightness.[4]

Both John Calvin and the psalmist testify that there are many things that can lead us to an experience of the beauty of the world: a deer silhouetted against evening shadows, a lily unfolding a perfect white flower, a limb reaching gently across a stream, a mountain peak with fresh snow glistening in the morning light. All of these images, and many more, can touch our souls with the lovely handiwork of a glorious Creator.

Now, bear in mind that all these things that can amaze our senses were also available for the Israelites to experience. If anything, our own amazement should be greater. After all, modern scientific instruments allow us not only to reach out to the edges of space but also to penetrate the center of living cells. Recall some of the colorful pictures taken by the Hubble telescope, floating silently above the earth; or picture those DNA strands revealed by electron microscopes. Whether in the far reaches of space or deep within our bones, an intricate interweaving of created reality testifies to the beauty of the universe and to the glory of the God who made it.

But let's be honest about it: if we are to look at the whole picture, we must admit that not everything in this world is beautiful. For instance, few people seem to attach the word *beautiful* to that intricate, well-designed organism that is called a scorpion! The same is true for others of God's creatures. Snakes inspire fear, and tarantulas suggest danger. Floodwaters and volcanic eruptions induce foreboding rather than delight, fear rather than pleasure. Even worse is the sadness that comes in the face of the disfigurement and pain that disease can inflict on a person.

Sometimes what we experience in this created world can be disheartening rather than uplifting. We will talk more about that later in this book. Here, however, we are focusing on the positive side, on the awareness of how captivating creation can be. For when it is captivating, when we rejoice in the beauty of the world as did the psalmist, then aren't we moved to look beyond this created order? Aren't we inclined to cast our gaze heavenward, to adore the One who fashioned it all? That, at least, is what the psalmist did:

> Bless the LORD, O my soul,
>   O LORD my God, you are very great. . . .
> I will sing to the LORD as long as I live;
>   I will sing praise to my God while I have being.
> May my meditation be pleasing to him,
>   for I rejoice in the LORD."
>
> (Ps. 104:1, 33–34)

Wisdom in Creation

Like Psalm 104, other passages in the Psalms recall the motifs of creation that we have seen in Genesis. Psalm 33, for instance, emphasizes that the Lord has created with authority, breathing out the world by the words of God's mouth: "By the word of the LORD the heavens were made, and all their host by the breath of his mouth" (v. 6). Psalm 74:12–17 describes in some detail how God has produced order out of chaos, giving structure and harmony to what would otherwise be disorder and discord. With the wisdom tradition in Israel, something new is added.

What is the "wisdom tradition"? For starters, it is the name given to the group of writings in the Old Testament that includes Proverbs, Job, and Ecclesiastes, as well as other writings such as the Wisdom of Jesus Ben Sirach (or Ecclesiasticus) in the books we call the Apocrypha. These writings seem to have developed in the context of the courts of the kings. There, the wise men, or sages, reflected on the world and the Torah. A very important role was giving instruction to the children of the nobility, and the sages even seem to have carried on conversations with their peers at other royal courts in the Near East.

In their thinking and theologizing about this mysterious world, the sages added a new thought. It is pronounced clearly and succinctly in Proverbs 3:19–20:

> The LORD *by wisdom* founded the earth;
>   by understanding he established the heavens;
>   by his knowledge the deeps broke open,
>   and the clouds drop down the dew.
>   (Italics added)

As you may know, the Greek word for "wisdom" is *sophia*. In Hebrew, the word is *hokmah*. We translate both of these words into English as "wisdom," but they have rather different connotations. The Greeks tended to understand "wisdom" somewhat theoretically and abstractly. They developed the discipline we call "philosophy" (the "love of wisdom"). Philosophical wisdom is interested in such things as the unity, the origin, and the meaning of the world. It asks questions like these: Can everything that exists be reduced to one substance? Is the world eternal or was it created? Is there a purpose guiding the world, or is everything ultimately governed by chance?

In Israel, the interest in wisdom is much more practical in nature. Not that the sages did not formulate answers to these kinds of questions. They did. Obviously, the sages held some rather definite views on the origin of the world, the purpose guiding it, and so forth. But they were not captivated by theoretical reflections on these issues. Rather, they were much more interested in the impact of wisdom on everyday life.

About as speculative as the sages become when talking about *hokmah*, or wisdom, is in the beautiful section in Proverbs 8:22–31, where we read, "The LORD created me at the beginning of his work, the first of his acts of long ago" (v. 22). The verses continue rehearsing how wisdom was with God prior to each creative act and how wisdom rejoiced along with God, as the Lord brought this structured, harmonious, glorious universe into being. Wisdom is personified here as though it is a personal being. Then, through much of the Proverbs, this personified Wisdom speaks wise words and offers wise counsel to the hearers or readers.

Now notice what Wisdom recommends to us. It is precisely, first, that people should live in reliance on God. As Proverbs 9:10 puts it: "The fear of the LORD is the beginning of wisdom." Second, people should follow the instruction and commandments of the Torah. That is to say, human lives should reflect the orderliness and harmony of creation itself. We should live our lives in an orderly, harmonious way and, therefore, in an *ethical* manner.

To put it very specifically: Why should we be good? Because it is the smartest, the wisest, way to live life. The sages conclude that to fit in with the structures of God's world makes more sense and is healthier for us than to kick against, violate, or ignore them. The sages understood what our society often forgets: that the commandments and the call to righteous living were not imposed by a God who wished to assert divine authority over a subservient, frail humanity. They were not given by a God who issues commands just because God can. Rather, the Lord God wants to provide knowledge and guidance about how human beings can live wisely and well.

We said a moment ago that wisdom can be personified almost as a being that stands in relation to God. This personal sense becomes even stronger in the New Testament. It hovers behind the language the apostle Paul uses in Colossians, when he searches for a way to describe the mystery and depths of the crucified Jewish carpenter, Jesus Christ, who has come from God to redeem humanity. For Paul, Alan Richardson writes, "the wisdom of God is most manifestly operative in what Christ did and was."[5] As Proverbs 8 could speak of Wisdom's presence and participation in God's creative acts, Paul writes of Christ, "He is the image of the invisible God, the firstborn of all creation; for in him all things in heaven and on earth were created . . . all things have been created through him and for him. He himself is before all things, and in him all things hold together" (Col. 1:15–17).

Does this perhaps sound similar to the beginning of the Gospel of John? There we read that the Word was with God in the beginning, and "all things came into being through him" (John 1:3). Jesus Christ, according to these writings, is God's personal Word and Wisdom. Christ is the agent and the sustainer of creation, which means that God's creative power is profoundly personal. Mystery of mysteries, it is truly God in person who is acting in creation.

The Perfection of Creation

As good as creation is, however, something better is still to come. That something is a "new" creation. As we saw, there are broken components in this world. The defects and tragic elements keep popping up, like weeds that simply won't die. Fortunately, the thrilling words in chapter 65 of the prophet Isaiah point us toward an ultimate completion of creation:

> For I am about to create new heavens
>   and a new earth; . . .
> . . . be glad and rejoice forever
>   in what I am creating;
> for I am about to create Jerusalem as a joy,
>   and its people as a delight. . . .
> no more shall the sound of weeping be heard in it,
>   or the cry of distress.
> No more shall there be in it
>   an infant that lives but a few days,
>   or an old person who does not live out a lifetime;
> for one who dies at a hundred years will be considered a youth.
>   (Isa. 65:17–20)

The words "new heavens and a new earth" take us right back to the first words in Genesis. They convey a sense of how original, how fresh, and how magnificent God's new works will be.

Isaiah's prophetic vision, however, was limited. If you look closely, you will note that the whole picture is still a bit "this-worldly." That is to say, the vision offers us a portrait of what this natural world, with all the imperfections removed, would look like. No dangers will threaten. No suffering will cause harm. No children will live but a few days. Nevertheless, they will probably die at one hundred or so. The picture, in other words, is still somewhat limited. The vision of a new world is not yet as great as it can be. What we have come to know as eternal, or everlasting, life is not yet part of this marvelous vision.

We go to the final prophetic book in the Scriptures to get that further vision. Revelation 21 also speaks of a "new heaven and a new earth" (v. 1). This time, though, the seer envisions even greater glories: death shall be "no more." Mourning, crying, and pain shall be "no more." All the former things—particularly the troublesome, tragic things—will have passed away (v. 4). In comforting and encouraging words, a Voice rings out from the throne:

> See, the home of God is among mortals.
> He will dwell with them;
> they will be his peoples,
> and God himself will be with them;
> he will wipe every tear from their eyes.
> (Rev. 21:3–4)

This is the ultimate vision. It is a vision of a creation restored, or better, recreated, to a level of magnificence that is beyond our comprehension. If the world is intended to be enjoyed in its present state, imagine the joy that will rise in our hearts in this new, incomprehensible world! Truly, the world is a mysterious, awesome creation of a marvelous God. And the mysterious, the awesome, reality of this creation has only just begun.

Chapter 2

Covenant

After setting the stage of human history in the first eleven chapters, Genesis next focuses on the primary ancestors of the people of Israel: the "patriarchs"—Abraham, Isaac, and Jacob—along with their wives and children. Recounting their meanderings through the land of Palestine, Genesis tells stories both comic and tragic. At the core of it all, however, these stories promise an unconditional relationship with God. First made with Abraham, the covenant is expanded with Israel under Moses at Mount Sinai. The covenant embodies a solemn divine oath that binds God to stand by this people forever; it calls them to be obedient to the Law; and it assures them that they can truly trust this God.

It is a very special day in the life of church: a baptism is taking place. A covenant is being sealed. The minister speaks words similar to these:

> Obeying the word of our Lord Jesus and confident of his promises, we baptize those whom God has called. In baptism God claims us, and seals us to show that we belong to God. God frees us from sin and death, uniting us with Jesus Christ in his death and resurrection.[1]

Covenant promises frame our lives:

> "I promise to uphold the Boy Scout law."
> "I promise before God and these witnesses to be your loving and faithful wife."
> "I promise to be a faithful minister, proclaiming the good news in Word and Sacrament, teaching faith, and caring for people."
> "I solemnly swear to tell the truth, the whole truth, and nothing but the truth."

Without question, covenants play a central role in defining who we are. The covenant concept plays a similar central role in Scripture by defining who we are as God's people. Old Testament scholar Walter Brueggemann goes so far as to say that *covenant* is perhaps "the central and defining theological affirmation of the Old Testament."[2]

But what exactly is a covenant? And why are covenants so important? The word *covenant* itself comes from the Latin word, *convenir,* which means "to come with or to agree." When we make a covenant with someone, we are literally saying to them, "I will come with you." This definition provides the foundation for the Old Testament understanding of what it means to be the people of God. We see this clearly in the Hebrew word for covenant, *berith,* which means "fetter" or "bond." Two parties are "tied together" by a binding agreement. The *B'nai Berith* are the "people of the covenant," those who are tied to God by a covenant. God promises to come with them, and they promise to go with God. The covenant between them exists to define the relationship and the obligations to which the parties are committing themselves.

In other words, covenants regulate the behavior of the participating parties. A covenant introduces trust and predictability. Nations make covenants in the form of peace treaties and territorial agreements; marriages are defined by wedding vows; the loyalty of people to nations, clubs, tribes, or societies is sealed by their pledges of allegiance.

A Covenanting God

The story of the Old Testament is the story of how the covenant between God and God's people plays out. Beginning in Genesis, the covenant concept is revealed in God's promises to certain representatives of the people: to Noah; to Abraham and the other patriarchs; to Moses, David, and Jeremiah. The Old Testament tells the story of God's faithfulness to the covenant and the people's unfaithfulness; it tells of promises kept and promises broken.

To understand the meaning of covenant in Scripture, therefore, we must begin with God, because the covenant is God's idea. It is God who establishes it. It is God who defines its terms. It is God who remains faithful to it. The covenant is rooted in God's faithfulness, trustworthiness, and steadfast love.

The Hebrew language has a special word for that trustworthy covenant love, *hesed.* This rich word is usually translated as "steadfast love," "loving-kindness," or "mercy." It expresses the patience of God in keeping covenant with Israel, even when Israel is unfaithful. The Psalter makes frequent use of the word *hesed*, as in this verse:

> I have not hidden your saving help within my heart,
>   I have spoken of your faithfulness and your salvation;
> I have not concealed your steadfast love (*hesed*) and your faithfulness
>   from the great congregation.

(Ps. 40:10)

The amazing essence of the covenant is that God *chooses* to become our friend. Our obedience to the covenant, therefore, is not to be based on an impersonal sense of duty but is to be a heartfelt, grateful response to a personal God who has entered into a genuine relationship with us. We are reminded of this in Psalm 25:14:

> The friendship of the LORD is for those who fear him,
> and he makes his covenant known to them.

It is this personal relationship with God that sets the biblical covenant apart from all other covenants: business agreements, sorority pledges, even marriage vows. A biblical covenant is a legal transaction in which God is a partner. What an incredible happening! Our God agrees to be tied to us, to come with us. Our God is not a God who set the planets in motion and wandered away, but "God with us," our friend. The Creator of the universe is willing to be our friend, to love us with steadfast love in spite of our falterings.

It is out of deep gratitude for this love that we make our covenant promise of trust and obedience. That trust enables us to move forward in complete confidence in God's steadfast love. That obedience means embodying the covenant in our lives, dedicating ourselves to being God's people in the world. This involves more than lip service or empty ritual. It is an active call to incorporate the demanding covenant concepts of righteousness and justice into all our actions. It is easy to see how Jesus' understanding of the kingdom of God was based on the foundation laid by the covenant. The twin requirements of trust and obedience are illustrated by two important Old Testament covenants.

The Covenant with Abraham: Trust

The first major expression of the covenant concept was the covenant with Abraham, renewed several times with Abraham's descendants. This covenant is the most often repeated covenant in the Old Testament. God speaks to Abraham six times in chapters 12–17 of Genesis, and in chapter 18, God says,

> I will not hide from Abraham what I am going to do. His descendants will become a great and mighty nation, and through him I will bless all the nations. I have chosen him in order that he may command his descendants to obey me and to do what is right and just. If they do, I will do everything for him that I have promised.
>
> (Gen. 18:17–19, paraphrased)

God's covenant with Abraham begins with a specific call that says, in essence, "Leave your native land, your relatives, and your father's home and go to a country that I am going to show you" (Gen. 12:1). Notice that this is what could be called a "unilateral covenant": a covenant of promise as opposed to a covenant of obligation. This means that God does all the promising. It is God who swears the oath, not Abraham. It is a covenant in which God alone is bound. Abraham says nothing at all. It is an astonishing example of free grace on God's part.

Yet, in Genesis 18, there is clearly a sense of God's expectations of Abraham in response to this grace: "that he may charge his children and his household after him to keep the way of the LORD by doing righteousness and justice" (v. 19). Abraham does not have to earn God's grace, but God expects a response of righteousness and justice to that grace. Abraham is also to teach "the way of the LORD" to his family and to his household. The covenant takes on reality only when Abraham demonstrates his trust in God in this way.

What we see reflected in this covenant is God's intention to form a special people, a family, a nation that belongs to God in a trusting relationship. We will discuss this in more detail in chapter 3, "The People of God." God promises to create this great nation from Abraham's descendants and to give them a special land to occupy. God promises "an everlasting covenant" (Gen. 17:7), one that can last forever because it is grounded in God's will, not in human promises.

All Abraham had to do was to obey God's call, to leave behind all that was familiar and venture into the unknown. A central issue in this covenant is trust. Can Abraham trust God? Can God trust Abraham? In his provocative book on the role of Abraham in the three major world religions, author Bruce Feiler writes:

> To be a descendant of Abraham is . . . to glance back at your native land, to peer ahead to your nameless destination, and to wonder, Do I have the courage to make the leap? Abraham makes the leap and thus secures his reputation for all time. The text is so matter-of-fact it almost masks the significance: "Abram

went forth as the Lord had commanded him." He does so silently, joining the covenant with his feet, not his words. The wandering man does what he does best, he walks. Only now he walks with God. And by doing so, Abraham leaves an indelible set of footprints: He doesn't *believe in* God; he *believes* God. He doesn't *ask for* proof; he *provides* the proof.[3]

The call of God was not just to Abraham. Through him a whole people was called into a new sense of identity. Just as the rainbow was the sign of the covenant with Noah (Gen. 9:12–13), so circumcision became the sign of the covenant with Abraham, an identifying marker of God's people. It was a symbol of trust in the promise, of entrance into the covenant, just as baptism is for us today.

Abraham's trusting response is mentioned several times in the New Testament, notably in Romans 4:20 ("No distrust made him waver concerning the promise of God"), Galatians 3:6 ("Just as Abraham 'believed God, and it was reckoned to him as righteousness'"), and the well-known passage in Hebrews 11: "By faith Abraham obeyed" (v. 8). God chose to become Abraham's friend, and Abraham responded to God's call with trust. Nancy Byrd Turner's poem "When Abraham Went Out of Ur" describes that trust by saying that Abraham

> bowed himself to his loved earth, and rent
> his garments, crying he could not go . . . and went.[4]

The problem with God's people is that we are not always like Abraham. God calls us into the unknown and we do not act with the same trust Abraham showed. Most of us stand at the edge of the desert and refuse to trust God's love and promises. God calls us to be a covenant people, living in a special trusting relationship with the One who wants to be our friend. To answer that call, we have only to "trust and obey" as an old hymn says, and then venture forth with confidence in the One who is always trustworthy.

The Covenant with Moses: Obedience

It is impossible to discuss the concept of covenant without examining its role in the life of God's people during the exodus from Egypt at the end of the patriarchal period. This chronological period finds them in the wilderness on the way to the land promised to them by God in the covenant with Abraham.

As we have seen, that covenant was a call from God to a particular people chosen and set apart by God. The covenant with Moses plays a different role. It gives shape and definition to that call by defining the responsibilities that accompany this unique relationship with God. Unlike the "unilateral" covenant of grace with Abraham, the covenant with Moses is "bilateral." It tells not only what God will do for the chosen people, but it spells out what they in turn should do for God. The people's responsibilities are defined in a set of rules known as the Law, or Torah, that describes in minute detail how they are to live as God's people.

The core of the covenant promise is found in the phrase "You shall be my people, and I will be your God" (Jer. 30:22). What a wonderful assurance: the promise of belonging! But there's a catch. It's great to belong: to be accepted into a sorority, to be adopted, to enter into a marriage, to become a citizen, to become a member of the church. However, every one of us knows that when we make the promises that accompany "belonging," we also accept certain responsibilities. We must take seriously the question "What does it mean to belong . . . to this family, this sorority, this marriage, this country, this church, this God?" The answer to that question is simply this: you play by the rules. If you truly want to belong, then you accept certain givens: to be a loving and faithful spouse; to obey the Girl Scout laws; to uphold the laws of your adopted country. Becoming the people of God also entails responsibilities that require obedience. Without a definition of these responsibilities, the idea of belonging becomes meaningless.

By defining the covenant relationship and its responsibilities, the law became a centripetal force uniting a group of assorted tribes that were quite likely to spin off in all directions. The laws that governed the people, even the details of their everyday lives, bound them together in a powerful, cohesive unity. The authority of the covenant reminded them that God was their leader, ruler, and commander-in-chief. There was no separation of church and state. They lived by the knowledge that their law rested on God's revealed will. This assurance is echoed over and over again in the psalms:

> He is the LORD our God,
>> his judgments are in all the earth.
> He is mindful of his covenant forever,
>> of the word that he commanded, for a thousand generations,
> the covenant that he made with Abraham,
>> his sworn promise to Isaac,
> which he confirmed to Jacob as a statute,
>> to Israel as an everlasting covenant.
>
> (Ps. 105:7–10)

The purpose of the law is to define what being faithful to God means in daily life. Faithfulness results in obedience, not the other way around.

The best known part of the Mosaic covenant is the Decalogue, commonly known as the Ten Commandments. No other piece of Old Testament literature is as familiar to us—although when put to the test, few of us can name all ten of the commandments. Scholars have seen a similarity in the form of the Decalogue and the traditional form of treaties used by Israel's neighboring kingdoms. These treaties defined the relationship between a state and its vassals. They were a means of preserving peace in a world where the balance of power was constantly in jeopardy. These treaties had six characteristic parts:

1. The preamble: the identification of the king who gives the treaty, his titles, genealogy, and so on. This shows the treaty is a message from the sovereign ruler to the vassal.
2. The historical prologue: a description of the previous relationship of the two parties.
3. The stipulations: the obligations to which the vassal agrees in accepting the covenant.
4. The deposit and public reading: telling where the document is to be kept and when it is to be read in public.
5. The list of witnesses: sometimes including the gods of both states.
6. The blessings and curses: the goods that will come to the vassal for obedience, and the curses that will come from disobedience.

Three of these characteristics are clearly seen in the Decalogue:

1. There is a preamble: "I am the LORD your God" (Exod. 20:2). The sovereign ruler is identified as God.
2. There is a historical prologue describing the previous relationship between God and Israel: God is the One "who brought you out of the land of Egypt" (Exod. 20:2).
3. There are certain stipulations, such as the obligation found in many other treaties to have no relationship to other sovereigns. In the Decalogue this appears as "you shall have no other gods before me" (20:3). Other stipulations protect the interests of the sovereign, especially in matters that affect the peace of the sovereign's domain, such as rebellious children, murder, adultery, theft, lying, and false accusations. These stipulations are clearly evident in the rest of the Ten Commandments (vv. 12–17).

While the last three characteristics of secular treaties are not found in the Decalogue, they may be noted in other references to the covenant in the Pentateuch, Joshua, and Judges.

For instance, there is a reference to the provision for the deposit and public reading of the Law in Deuteronomy, when Moses places the tablets in the ark (Deut. 10:5) and commands the priests to read the Law "before all Israel" every seventh year during the festival of booths (31:10–11). Joshua appeals to the people as "witnesses against yourselves that you have chosen the LORD, to serve him" (Josh. 24:22). Deuteronomy 27 and 28 detail the curses that follow disobedience to the covenant Law and the blessings that will follow obedience.[5]

What sets the Decalogue apart from these other treaties is that it is not a covenant between nations but a covenant between God and God's people. Therefore, it is a covenant that places moral and theological considerations above political and economic ones. The most fascinating aspect of the Decalogue is that it consists of a few clear, simple basics that everyone can understand. They are still as pertinent today as they were in Moses' time. The commandments do not form a system that is too complex to be grasped or too suffocating to live out. Properly understood, they remain a code that protects the life of the community and gives it order and shape.

In the *Sabbath and Festival Prayer Book,* there is this remarkable description of the relationship of the covenant Law to Judaism:

> Our religion goes beyond the formulation of universal postulates and idealistic ends. It translates the poetry of moral aspiration into the prose of everyday life. It is a religion of behavior as well as of beliefs. It brings down the holy tablets from the heights of Sinai to the valley of decision and the plain of realization. It translates the Torah into life.[6]

But the Mosaic covenant is far more than just the Decalogue. It is found throughout the Pentateuch, the first five books of the Bible. When we examine the whole of it, we find many similarities to the covenant with Abraham. In fact, you could say that it is a particular covenant that defines the more general Abrahamic covenant. Both of the covenants contain promises to offspring and assurances that those offspring would be "God's own people." For example, Exodus 19:5 predicts that Israel will become a nation of priests and a holy nation. Exodus 6:7 says, "I will take you as my people, and I will be your God." First Peter quotes both of these promises in addressing "the new Israel" that had come into being through Christ:

> But you are a chosen race, a royal priesthood, a holy nation, God's own people, in order that you may proclaim the mighty acts of him who called you out of darkness into his marvelous light. Once you were not a people, but now you are God's people; once you had not received mercy, but now you have received mercy.
>
> (1 Pet. 2:9–10)

Christ and the New Covenant

Jesus states clearly in the Sermon on the Mount that he did not come to abolish the Law but to fulfill it (Matt. 5:17). His intent was to lead his people into an even deeper respect and understanding of the covenant requirements and a truer appreciation of what it means to be accepted and loved by God, to be a part of God's covenant family.

However, according to the Gospel writers, Jesus only uses the word *covenant* once. Both Mark and Luke tell us that at the Last Supper, he said as he held up the cup, "This is my blood of the covenant, which is poured out for many" (Mark 14:24; Luke 22:20). Paul alters these words slightly by quoting Jesus as saying, "This cup is the new covenant in my blood" (1 Cor. 11:25). These words are familiar to us because of their use in the celebration of the Eucharist. They remind us that as we share this special meal, we are acknowledging that we are bound together in a covenant relationship with God and one another. We are recognizing that we are indeed God's people, and that God is our God. For this we offer up to God our "Eucharist," our heartfelt thanksgiving.

The word *covenant* is used only thirty-three times in the New Testament, and half of these references are quotes from the Old Testament or references to Old Testament covenants. The idea of covenant, however, underlies another very important theological concept in the New Testament. As theologian Rachel Henderlite points out:

> When Jesus announced the kingdom of God, he made use of an expression that carried with it many rich meanings for the people to whom he spoke. The seed of the kingdom of God was in the covenant. The Hebrew nation knew God as its king, ruler of nature and history, and knew itself as a people chosen to be God's subjects. God had promised that they would be a blessed nation and a blessing to all nations. Thus they believed that God's rule extended to all people. They looked to a time when this sovereignty should be manifest in the whole world.[7]

However, Jesus did not identify the realm of God with the kingdom of Israel. When he announced that "the kingdom is at hand," he was affirming the basic conviction of his life—the rulership and righteous love of God. His understanding of this kingdom was difficult for the Jews to accept, and it is difficult for us as well. Even though we pray, "Thy kingdom come," are we really ready for it? Are we ready for a world ruled by a God of love? Are we ready to take our responsibilities in that kingdom? As Henderlite declares, God has chosen "not to work *on* us, but *in* us; not to do *to* us but *through* us."[8] The new covenant, like the old, takes on reality when we assume the obligations of trust and obedience that are a part of what it means to be God's people.

The paradox of the law is that although we need definitions of what it means to be the people of God, those very definitions remind us how far we fall short. However, being covenant people means we live in the light of grace. The same God who tells us clearly what kind of obedience is expected if we are to be covenant people freely forgives us when we fail and offers us hope and restoration.

It is not easy to speak of hope in today's world. Our minds are filled with pictures of terrorism, starvation, violence, and the threat of nuclear war. Our lives so quickly become pits of depression and frustration and emptiness. When everything seems to be working against us and against the values in which we believe, it is easy to turn aside from the covenant demands, as the Israelites did, or to turn them into burdensome yokes of legalism in a desperate search for security.

But we are a covenant people. And we have a covenant God. And God's promise to us is that in spite of our sin and disobedience and discouragement, the covenant stands firm. Because of God's real love for us, written in blazing letters not on tablets of stone but in our hearts, we have hope (see Jer. 31:31–34). And because we have hope, we rejoice in the covenant promises, as did the psalmist:

> The LORD is gracious and merciful.
> He provides food for those who fear him;
>   he is ever mindful of his covenant.
> The works of his hands are faithful and just;
>   all his precepts are trustworthy.
> They are established forever and ever,
>   to be performed with faithfulness and uprightness.
> He sent redemption to his people;
>   he has commanded his covenant forever.
>   (Ps. 111:4b–5, 7–9a)

Chapter 3

The People of God

In the period of the exodus and the wilderness wanderings, the descendents of Abraham gradually develop a new sense of identity. Led out of Egypt by God's mighty power, they accept God's commandments at Mount Sinai and agree to the religious, ethical, and social stipulations recorded in Exodus and the other "books of Moses" that make up the Torah. The purpose of all these rules and regulations is to bind this group together as a distinct people. To be God's people is to enjoy a place of great honor, but it also implies a great responsibility, for Israel is to demonstrate to the world God's intention that people live as a community in which all share with one another, out of love for one another.

The Old Testament looks back to the period of the exodus as the time when Israel became a nation, the people of God. Sometimes we refer to a collection of human beings as a "people." Not all collections, however, would qualify for that description. Some might be too small, and some too large. For instance, a group of Native Americans is usually not called a "people" but a "tribe." On the other end of the scale, the assemblage of human beings on the continent of Europe is not called a "people" either, but they are often called "peoples."

In the Old Testament, the Hebrew word *am* is translated by "people," and the Israelites are called the *am Yahweh*, the "people of God." In the Hebrew Scriptures it becomes clear that God intended, as part of the divine plan for salvation, to establish a particular people on the face of this earth. Why would the Lord God do that? What would such a people look like, and what would their purpose be? How would that people relate to God's plans and purposes for salvation? These are the kinds of questions that will guide us as we seek to understand better this theme.

The Origin of God's People

There are many theories not only about how the twelve tribes of Israel became one nation, or people, but also about how there came to be twelve tribes in the first place. Critical opinion in Old Testament studies assumes that Israel coalesced into one group in Palestine gradually, over a period of time. The stories of the ancestors, such as Abraham and Sarah, Isaac and Rebekah, and Jacob and Rachel (and Leah), were thus brought together to make one continuous history.

While, with many variations, this "evolutionary" view has won general assent in scholarship, the biblical narrative pictures Israel's origins simply as the result of a marvelous liberation of a whole people from bondage in Egypt. The constitutive moment when Israel becomes a "people" occurs in the events at Mount Sinai. There, God formally establishes the covenant through Moses. We considered the theme of "covenant" in the last chapter. Here we will be observing the relationship between God and human beings that is founded on the covenant motif.

Notice the beautiful imagery in Exodus 19, where the Lord reminds Israel how God has carried them out of the clutches of the Egyptians. God, we read, "bore [them] on eagles' wings" (Exod. 19:4) through the wilderness. Visualize the consolation implied in that image: in the midst of a dry and dangerous desert, the people of Israel were lifted up and made to soar across the sky to a place of safety and refuge. It would appear that the image caught Israel's imagination, because it reappears in places like Isaiah 40:31 and Deuteronomy 32:11. It also caught the imagination of Michael Joncas, who wrote a beloved song titled "On Eagles' Wings," based on Psalm 91.[1] That song has often brought inspiration when sung in worship, as well as comfort when sung at a memorial service. It may be worthwhile to pause for a moment to recall a time in your own life when God lifted you out of a troublesome situation as though on eagle's wings. If you do, can you remember the sense of relief and comfort you experienced at the time? Take a few moments to consider how that feeling may parallel the experience of the Israelites of old.

Immediately after God's reminder that Israel has been borne on eagles' wings, there comes a solemn promise related to the covenant:

> Now therefore, if you obey my voice and keep my covenant, you shall be my treasured possession out of all the peoples. Indeed, the whole earth is mine, but you shall be for me a priestly kingdom and a holy nation.
>
> (Exod. 19:5–6)

There are two primary items we should emphasize here. First is the focus on God as the Lord of all. When we talk about "the people of God," the main word to underscore is always *God*. Israel never exists by itself. Rather, it exists only and always as a people brought together by the Lord on the basis of the covenant, which we talked about in the last session. As an illustration of this, recall those famous words that Ruth says to her mother-in-law, Naomi: "Where you go, I will go; where you lodge, I will lodge; *your people* shall be my people, and *your God* my God" (Ruth 1:16, italics added).

Ruth recognizes the close interconnection between this people she has married into and the God they serve. Exodus 19 makes clear that the emphasis is on God's action. It is God who chooses this people, and there would be no people without God's choice. As though to assure that Israel gets this point, Exodus underlines God's power to choose: "Indeed, the whole earth is mine" (Exod. 19:5). That is to say, God rules; God reigns; God governs all people; God controls all the earth. Therefore, nothing—and no one—on earth can withstand the Lord.

The second item to notice is the fact that the word *am*, or "people," does not actually appear here. This is not unusual, because often other terms for Israel appear in the Old Testament Scriptures. For example, Israel is called a "house" or a "nation." Sometimes the phrase used is "sons" or "children," as in "the sons (or children) of Israel." At other times, words such as *congregation* or *assembly* occur. There are minor differences in nuance in these terms, but principally they are simply referring to this group that is God's people, Israel.

Here in Exodus, as we said, the word *people* is not used. The words we do find are *nation*, *possession,* and *kingdom.* Each of these terms implies something significant about this people. Note especially the word "*kingdom*." It does not stand alone in the text. What we read is that God will make Israel to be a "priestly kingdom," and this designation contains an important implication regarding Israel's purpose.

What is the function of a priest? What does a "priest" actually do? At the most basic level, a priest is a religious figure who serves as an intermediary between a god and human beings who worship that god. In the Old Testament, priests are the ones who officiate in the tabernacle in the wilderness and later in the Temple in Jerusalem. The Israelites did not approach their God directly to offer sacrifices and offerings, but rather they brought them to the priests, who made the offerings on their behalf. In a sense, then, priests provide access to God, an access that would otherwise be at best suspect.

Now Exodus declares that Israel is to be a "priestly kingdom." This people will serve as an intermediary for other peoples. This nation will provide access to God for other nations. Recall the promise of the covenant made to Abraham, which we considered in the last chapter. One of the promises was that "in you all the families of the earth shall be blessed" (Gen. 12:3). Here that same covenantal promise is broadened to all of Abraham's descendents. The whole nation is to serve a priestly role: it will be the instrument by which God's blessings reach the entire world.

While God's purpose in establishing Israel was not simply to bless them as an individual people, it was easy for Israel to take pride in its status as a chosen nation or a priestly kingdom. In their place, it would be easy for us to do so too. The temptation to hold onto blessings, honors, or privileges lies close at hand for all of us. Frequently, church fellowships have operated out of a sense that their way was the best, or truest, or most faithful way—and sometimes the *only* right way—to worship God. From the outside, it is easy to see signs of pridefulness and feelings of superiority in such groups. Not so easy to see, of course, are such signs in our own groups or our own attitudes.

Another term used for Israel—and one that has a venerable history in the later Christian church—is the word *election*. The people of Israel are God's elect, or chosen, people. This term has often been taken to imply some kind of privilege or special favor. That is not wrong, of course, for being chosen by God is surely a great, even a supreme, privilege. The point, however, is that privilege is only one half of the equation. To put it in theological terms, election is not only for privilege but also for a task. The second half of the equation is service. For Israel, God's wonderful blessing in making them a priestly kingdom means that they are commissioned with the high responsibility of extending God's grace and love to all peoples. There can be joy and thankfulness in being given such a task, but there is no room to become prideful about it.

The Life of God's People

Chapter 19 in Leviticus gives us a good idea of what a "people"—especially God's people—ought to look like. You will recognize that verse 18 is the source of Jesus' reply when he is asked about the greatest commandment in Matthew 22:35–40. Jesus responds by underscoring two commandments from the Old Testament. First, Jesus quotes Deuteronomy 6:5, "You shall love the LORD your God." Then he quotes this verse from Leviticus: "You shall love your neighbor as yourself."

It is important to notice the sorts of things that this chapter in Leviticus considers important in loving our neighbor. We find that especially in verses 9–18. When you reap your field, says the text, leave some of the produce for those who are poor and for those who are aliens. Echoes of the Ten Commandments sound when we hear the words "Do not steal." "Do not swear falsely." And principles of justice and equity surface powerfully in commands not to be partial or to render unjust judgments.

Underlying these verses is a clear message about what the attitude of God's people ought to be. To put it in negative terms, Israel's spirit ought not to be defined by words such as *holding* and *keeping*, *grasping* and *clutching*, *clinging* and *clenching*. Rather, the spirit of Israel should show itself in words such as *distributing* and *supplying*, *donating* and *giving*. In short, their attitude should be one of sharing what they have with others.

If you have had the opportunity to travel in foreign countries, you have probably noticed a rather common phenomenon. Particularly when visiting third-world countries like those in Latin America or Africa or Asia, many travelers observe that people in these nations seem so inclined to give or to share whatever they have. Hospitality often seems to be uppermost in these people's minds and hearts, even at times when giving and sharing would appear (to us from the West) to be detrimental to their physical welfare. When you visit a country whose people have been brought close to starvation due to famine or drought, it is a humbling experience to receive a hearty welcome into a home and to find a table set with abundant gifts of food.

This is what Leviticus is enjoining on Israel. Like those open-handed and open-hearted people in third-world countries, God is instructing Israel to live as a people that, above all else, cares for each other. In the experience of the exodus, unfortunately, Israel often did not act like the caring, sharing people that God intended. On more than one occasion, the people promised their loyalty with words like those in Exodus 24:7: "All that the LORD has spoken we will do, and we will be obedient." When they left the heights of their mountaintop experiences, however, they found that the promises they had made were hard to keep. Life in the everyday round of planting and harvesting, buying and selling, caring, sharing, and loving, was just too much for them. The people had high hopes and high ideals, but—as the pithy phrase puts it, somewhat ironically—"life intervened."

Israel's problem was at root one that all peoples before and all those after them have shared. It is simply *sinfulness*. We will talk about this in more detail in the next chapter. Here we need note only that sin is a kind of infection that affects us all, regularly and continually. It is hoped that it does not ravage us, but it can never be completely eliminated either. The Scriptures make it clear that sin has its effects not only on us as individuals but also on us as a corporate body, a "people." At various times for Israel, this affliction became overwhelming. At those times, prophets like Isaiah and Jeremiah or Micah and Malachi rose up to protest the cancer that was swallowing up God's people.

The Obligations of God's People

It is generally agreed that Amos is the first prophet whose words were recorded. This set a precedent for writing down the message of God's prophets when they rebuked the people for their failures. Amos served what appears to have been a brief stint as a prophet in the eighth century B.C. By that time, the people had settled in the land of Palestine, judges had come and gone, and a kingdom had been established. The glory days under Saul, David, and Solomon had not lasted long, however, and the kingdom had soon broken apart into two sections. The northern portion continued to call itself Israel, while the southern portion adopted the name Judah.

Some two centuries after the division of the kingdom, Amos travels north from his home in Judah to Israel, carrying a word of the Lord:

> Hear this word that the LORD has spoken against you, O people of Israel, against the whole family that I brought up out of the land of Egypt: You only have I known of all the families of the earth; therefore I will punish you for all your iniquities.
>
> (Amos 3:1–2)

Notice how Amos emphasizes that the people redeemed from bondage in Egypt are one "family." Judah and Israel belong together; and Amos recognizes that their split is already a sign of their failure. As a people they ought to be characterized by caring and sharing, but tragically they are alienated and at enmity with one another. Thus, the prophet is not lashing out against the northern kingdom, Israel, as though the southern kingdom, Judah, were home free! *Both* sections of the *whole* people have to bear their own share of guilt.

Nevertheless, Amos has been sent by the Lord to confront Israel particularly. Amos 2:6-7 gives us the first cut, and a kind of summary, of the prophet's accusations against Israel:

> Thus says the LORD:
> For three transgressions of Israel,
>   and for four, I will not revoke the punishment;
> because they sell the righteous for silver,
>   and the needy for a pair of sandals—
> they who trample the head of the poor into the dust of the earth,
>   and push the afflicted out of the way.

Kinds of actions that are supportive and should characterize relationships among this people are violated in various directions here. The line that stands out is the dismal comment that "they sell the needy for a pair of sandals." Sandals are a humble part of a person's attire, and they are worn on one's feet. How sad that fair treatment for a poor person should be judged to be so insignificant. The nation, Amos charges, is no longer marked by an attitude of sharing. The prevailing spirit has become a concern only to "get what I can for myself."

It would be a relief to think that Amos's situation was unique. It would be comforting to see his time as an anomaly in the history of God's people. Unfortunately, many of the other prophets in the Hebrew Scriptures make similar charges against the people of Israel. Likewise, we can easily point to countless examples of the same deplorable injustice and cold indifference in other lands and in different ages—not least in our own age and our own land!

You may wish to take a few moments to reflect on ways in which Amos's words might apply to the treatment of the less fortunate in our society. Where might the poor be "sold for a pair of shoes"? How might those who are more fortunate be "trampling the poor into the dust"?

The Essence of God's People

God's people under the old covenant were united by blood—by an ethnic, racial identity. This basic unity was meant to be coupled with something much more profound: an interior faith in the God of Israel. Frequently, however, this kind of ethnic unity was equated solely with the externals of physical lineage and observance of regulations of the Torah. It was easy enough to presume that individual Israelites were favored by God simply because they were part of this people. By the time of the New Testament, the concept of an ethnic people of God had hardened to the point that the Jews set themselves apart from all other nations and peoples. Those other groups could be lumped together in a single, usually contemptuous term *Gentiles.*

E. P. Sanders points out in *Jesus and Judaism* that, given the atmosphere around the first century, there was no love lost on the part of the Jewish people for Gentiles. Still, the little evidence that is available from rabbinic sources, he says, makes it likely that "most Jews who thought about the matter one way or the other would have expected many Gentiles to turn to the Lord when his glory was revealed."[2]

Nevertheless, with the appearance of Jesus Christ, some eight centuries after the time of Amos, a more inward and inclusive turn takes place for the conception of God's people. No passage from the New Testament expresses this more powerfully and succinctly than does Galatians 3:26–29. These few verses from Paul's epistle summarize in a programmatic way what God's people will look like in this new covenantal arrangement:

> For in Christ Jesus you are all children of God through faith. As many of you
> as were baptized into Christ have clothed yourselves with Christ. There is no
> longer Jew or Greek, there is no longer slave or free, there is no longer male
> and female; for all of you are one in Christ Jesus. And if you belong to Christ,
> then you are Abraham's offspring, heirs according to the promise.
>
> (Gal. 3:26–29)

Notice how central baptism is to all the points that are made here. For God's
original people, it was physical birth into the nation of Israel that made a person part of the people of God. In this new era, the defining characteristic has
become the sacrament of baptism in the name of Father, Son, and Holy Spirit.
It is this sign, and this sign alone, that procures membership into God's people. Baptism illustrates acceptance of God's gift of salvation in Jesus Christ.
And since baptism through faith in Christ is the defining characteristic, other
qualifications such as gender (neither male nor female), nationality (neither
Jew nor Greek), and social status (neither slave nor free) no longer count.

At least, they shouldn't count! Often enough in the earliest Christian com-
munities, the implications of Paul's words went unrecognized. In Acts 15, for
example, we read how the apostles gathered for what has come to be called
the "first church council," in order to debate a heated issue: Can Gentiles join
the church without first taking on all the regulations of Judaism? A little later,
Paul was forced to deal with distress in one of his own churches, one in which
he himself had lived for eighteen months. In Corinth, the church had divided
along various lines—relationships to particular apostles, ability to exercise
spiritual gifts, and the like. Paul was forced to confront in none-too-pleasant
terms their prideful ambitions and arrogant attitudes.

Not recognizing equality in Christ through baptism seems to have been
common in these early congregations. To cite one more example, the letter of
James also addresses issues of social status that arose in gatherings of Christian congregations. The letter has strong words to say about favoritism of the
rich over the poor:

> If a person with gold rings and in fine clothes comes into your assembly,
> and if a poor person in dirty clothes also comes in, and if you take notice of
> the one wearing the fine clothes and say, "Have a seat here, please," while
> to the one who is poor you say, "Stand there," or, "Sit at my feet," have you
> not made distinctions among yourselves and become judges with evil
> thoughts? . . . You have dishonored the poor.
>
> (James 2:2–4, 6)

Early Christians did not easily and always look past distinctions such as
class, race, gender, and even spirituality as they sought to live in this new

arrangement of God's people called the church. And centuries of practice have not necessarily made members of the church more accepting of one another.

Perhaps this problem is due partially to the fact that outward distinctions are so much more concrete than is our unity in Jesus Christ. This brings us back to the topic of baptism, for it is this sacrament that portrays our unity with all people everywhere who bear Christ's name. In a sense, through baptism, everyone "looks alike." Paul's words to the Galatians are: you have "clothed yourselves" in Christ. This language gained special meaning in the early church, for it was a frequent custom to provide new garments to those who were baptized. New converts would sometimes remove their old clothes before stepping into the baptismal font. As they came up out of the font, they would be wrapped in new, white clothes, signifying their new life in Christ.

Now we are touching on the deepest level of what the theme of "the people of God" entails. It is oneness in Christ Jesus, a oneness that is based on faith in God's grace. That oneness and that faith are both witnessed outwardly as we are baptized and clothed in Christ. Over and above all the other differentiations that we experience in everyday life, this foundation in Christ is meant to draw us together in a unity too deep for words. But theologians like to use words. Thus, they use phrases like "mystical unity" and "communion of saints" to express this profound theological reality.

You probably recognize the phrase "communion of saints" as one of the parts of the Apostles' Creed. It occurs in the third section of the creed, which focuses on realities of faith connected to the Holy Spirit:

I believe in the Holy Ghost (or Spirit),
the holy catholic Church,
the communion of saints,
the forgiveness of sins,
the resurrection of the body,
and the life everlasting. Amen.

Confessing that the church is a "communion of saints" emphasizes the deep unity among those who are part of the church, those who carry the name of Christ. That unity reaches down into the profound identity by which we are united to Jesus. By the power of the Spirit, we are brought together in a caring, sharing communion that goes far beyond racial, ethnic, or familial bonds. The words of the old hymn capture the reality well:

In Christ there is no east or west, In Him no south or north;
But one great fellowship of love, Throughout the whole wide earth.[3]

Chapter 4

Sin

After a lengthy sojourn in the wilderness, according to the book of Joshua, the people of Israel settle in the land of Palestine. At first there is no centralized rule, and the period of the "judges" sees the rise of a number of leaders who take command in times of national emergency. The people find it hard to live up to the weighty promises they had made earlier. Thus, they are frequently unfaithful, both to God and to the community in which they live. The failures of the people lead to suffering and sorrow, and the resulting distress leads in turn to an awareness of sin and error. Through these experiences, the people are forced to face their failures and to approach the Lord God in repentance.

There they were—the people of God—called and set apart and blessed by God, settling into a land of milk and honey, promising to keep the covenant vows they had made to walk in God's ways. And they failed. Miserably. Spectacularly. Over and over again. And so do we.

Throughout the Word, sin snakes its way into the lives of God's people, leaving its ugly mark of rebellion and defiance, of arrogance and violence, of hate and destruction. Sin has been defined by John Calvin as "not our nature, but its derangement";[1] by Reinhold Niebuhr as "rebellion against God";[2] and by Walter Brueggemann as "the violation of God's will for that world of well-being willed by the creator God."[3]

All these definitions say something very important about sin. But perhaps we understand sin best when it takes on flesh and blood in descriptions of a mother in Kosovo or Palestine keening over the body of her child, in photographs of despairing refugees fleeing enemy attacks on their villages, in news reports of mass murderers leaving behind a trail of bodies in school yards and other public places, in the awful reality of September 11, 2001. Such violence, such senseless slaughter, seems to us incomprehensible, unreal, and *sinful*. We shudder and ask ourselves: How could anybody *do* those dreadful things to other human beings? Sin is easy to spot when it makes headlines with blood-baths and rotting corpses, with corporate crime and adultery in high places.

The problem with sin is that it is not limited to such flagrant misdeeds. It affects all of us "good people" who presumably hold to the "solid family values" that politicians love to praise. Most of us give intellectual assent to the phrase "All have sinned," but we tend to qualify it privately with the phrase "except me, of course." Or at least we find ways to justify our "sinful" behavior, make excuses for ourselves, and get by on the notion that we're not so bad after all in compar-ison with mass murderers and sociopathic snipers and terrorists.

The biblical testimony is that sin is real. Sin is pervasive. Sin is prevalent. Sin is crippling and debilitating. Sin keeps us from being the people of God. Sin prevents us from living up to our part of the covenant. In short, we would do well to heed Walter Brueggemann's warning: "Sin is serious business and has serious, practical, discernible consequences."[4]

The historical books of the Hebrew Bible could be described as catalogs of sin. The cycle of sin in Judges, the sins of the kings of both the northern and southern kingdoms, and the apostasy of the people as they worshiped other gods are given specificity in the stories of particular individuals. There is Saul, who plotted evil against David (1 Sam. 23:9), and David, who "despised" the Lord (2 Sam.12:9) when he had Uriah killed in order to take his wife. Sin is person-ified by Ahab, who "sold himself to do what was evil in the sight of the LORD, urged on by his wife Jezebel" (1 Kings 21:25), and wicked Queen Athaliah, who tried to destroy all the royal family (2 Kings 11:1). The list of kings is punctu-ated by the phrase "he did what was evil in the sight of the LORD."

So just what is sin? To understand sin from a biblical perspective, it is help-ful to know something about the meaning of the word in the original languages.

Categories of Sin

The Old Testament authors seldom gave theoretical definitions of sin. Instead, they defined it by its effects. Sin is basically understood as rebellion against God, but under this umbrella heading, it is possible to distinguish several gen-eral categories.

The first is the ethical category: *sin as failure.* The ethical terms for sin used in Scripture denote the failure to do what is generally perceived as good and right. The most frequently used Hebrew word expressing this failure is *chatah,* which means literally "to miss the mark." That is to say, it usually has the sense of erroneous action or making a mistake, rather than sin in a deeply religious sense. This is the word used when Abimelech asks Abraham, "How have I sinned against you?" (Gen. 20:9).

A good illustration of *chatah* is found in Proverbs 19:2: "Desire without knowledge is not good, and one who moves too hurriedly misses the way." *Chatah* takes on a religious usage when it is employed to indicate that there *is* a Way, an order, a pattern for our human relationship to God, and that often we "miss the way." An appropriate prayer of repentance is simply "Lord, I goofed."

The second is the psychological category: *sin as malicious evil.* A second Hebrew word, *awon*, describes acts that are deliberately evil or malicious. It is often translated "iniquity," a term seldom heard today outside church. The evil intent behind the Holocaust, the viciousness of mass murderers, and acts of terrorism can appropriately be described as *awon.* It is used far more often as a noun than as a verb, and it carries the idea of willful guilt.

The third is the theological category: *sin as defiance against God.* A highly significant Hebrew verb for sin is *pashah*, meaning "to revolt or rebel against a superior," or, in biblical terms, willful rebellion against God. It is a deeper and more serious kind of sin that just making a mistake or missing the mark, because it is, as theologian Rachel Henderlite has stated, "the refusal of God's love."[5] It is a recognition of this kind of defiant disobedience that produced the confession attributed to King David in Psalm 51: "Against you, you alone, have I sinned" (Ps. 51:4).

In summary, although the three categories are evident in the Old Testament, they are often used interchangeably. Often they are used in the same passage to reinforce the sense of disobedience to God. An example of this is found in Exodus 34:7, which uses words from all three categories to describe God's acts of "forgiving iniquity (*awon*) and transgression (*peshah*) and sin (*chatah*)."

In the Gospels, there are few direct references to sin. Alan Richardson comments, "Jesus neither speculated about sin nor explained what he understood by it. He simply reckoned with its reality."[6] However, where sin is mentioned, there are several categories of sinners in the New Testament as in the Old:

1. *The godless*: those who live in conscious contradiction to the law.
2. *The am ha-arets* (people of the land; about 80 percent of the population): those who do not observe the law strictly. These are referred to in Matthew 11:19, when Jesus was accused of being a friend of tax collectors and sinners.
3. Those who are separated from God. When Peter encountered Jesus, he referred to himself as being "a sinful man" (Luke 5:8).

The New Testament terms for sin are similar to those in the Old Testament. The Hebrew *chatah* is translated by the Greek word *hamartia*, which takes on a new level of conscious intention to go astray and oppose God. Here it is almost always a matter of an offense against God, with emphasis on one's guilt. It is used of individual acts, as in Peter's sermon in Acts 2:38: "Repent . . . so that your sins may be forgiven." It is used as a characteristic of human nature: "If we say that we have no sin, we deceive ourselves" (1 John 1:8). It is used also to describe a power that rules over us (Rom. 6:12), dwells in us (7:17), and to which we are slaves (6:16). *Anomia* carries the sense of contempt for God's law, and moral evil is denoted by *kakia*. The most deeply theological Greek word is *asebeia*, which means an offense against God.

The New Testament view of sin is expressed best in Romans 3:23: "All have sinned and fall short of the glory of God." We do not reflect the image of God in our behavior, and the awareness of that sets up the conflict Paul described in his well-known statement "I do not understand my own actions. For I do not do what I want, but I do the very thing I hate" (Rom. 7:15). However, the doctrine of sin in the New Testament is dominated by the assurance that Christ has come to conquer it. It is not the particular sin as such that is forgiven but the act of separation from God. The Lamb of God "takes away the sin of the world" (John 1:29).

One thing is clear about the scriptural understanding of sin: it is not normal. It is deviant behavior. It breaks the harmony of the covenant relationship between human beings and God, and because of that, it incurs God's displeasure. Sin alienates us from God; it is a revolt against the covenant itself. This is a basic concept in both the Old Testament and the New Testament understanding of sin.

Even though Scripture recognizes that sin is not normal, but deviant, it also acknowledges that we bear the seeds of sin in us. We refuse to be responsive to God's love and God's reign. In the words of Paul, "The evil I do not want is what I do" (Rom. 7:19). In the story of Noah, we read that "the wickedness of humankind was great in the earth, and that every inclination of the thoughts of their hearts was only evil continually" (Gen. 6:5). The essence of sin, then, is found not in isolated acts of transgression, but in the depths of our being: "in every inclination" of the thoughts of our hearts. This implies that because sin is rooted in the heart, all human life is liable to its taint. No area of life is exempt from it. The psalmist says "There is no one who does good. . . . They have all gone astray, they are all alike perverse; there is no one who does good, no, not one" (Ps. 14:1, 3). Presbyterian minister and author Frederick Buechner puts it succinctly: "Original sin means we all originate out of a sinful world which taints us from the word go. We all tend to make ourselves the center of the universe, pushing away centrifugally from that center, everything that seems to impede its freewheeling."[7]

Sin in the Period of the Judges

Nowhere is that "pushing away" more clearly shown than in the cyclical format of the book of Judges, with its rhythmic refrain: "Then the people . . . sinned against the LORD. . . . The LORD became furious . . . and let the enemies around overpower them. . . . They were in great distress. . . . The LORD gave the Israelites leaders who saved them . . . but the people would return to the old ways and behave worse than the previous generation."[8] This passage not only sums up the book of Judges; it sums up the history of Israel for over four hundred years. It can be summarized with four "R" words: Relapse, Retribution, Respite, and Return. And then the cycle begins again, with just a change of names of the leaders and the conquerors. The parade of leaders includes warriors and folk heroes, a wise woman, and the son of a prostitute: Othniel, Ehud, Shamgar, Deborah, Barak, Gideon, Abimelech, Tola, Jair, Jephthah, Ibzan, Elon, Abdon, and, finally, the best known, Samson.

It is easy to think of the Israelites as flagrant examples of ingratitude and backsliding, but we come nearer the truth of these stories when we see in them a mirror of ourselves. Their sins of rebelling against God to worship other gods are our sins as well. While Baal worship is not common today, there are contemporary gods just as powerful who command our allegiance. We worship Success and Recognition, Education and Degrees, Possessions and Bank Accounts, Genealogies and Social Status. We spend lavishly on $6,000 kitchen ranges and $100 ballgame tickets and begrudgingly drop $5 in the offering plate at church. Our sins are varied and complex, but no less real than the sins of the people in the period of the judges. Firm adherence to the covenant has been displaced by waffling indecision and lukewarm commitment.

That waffling brings on God's displeasure. It is hard sometimes for us to grasp the biblical truth that God's wrath is an integral part of God's love. God was angry with Israel because of that great love for them. We begin to understand that anger when we compare it to the feelings parents have when their own children go astray. The punishment that follows the sin shows God's love no less than the rewards that follow obedience.

At the turn of the century, Alexander MacLaren wrote these beautiful words that describe what we can learn about sin from the book of Judges:

> This miserable repetition of the same weary round of sin, punishment, respite and renewed sin, sets in a strong light the two great wonders of man's obstinate persistency in unfaithfulness and sin, and of God's unwearied persistency in discipline and patient forgiveness. His charity "suffers long and is kind, is not easily provoked." We can weary out all forbearance but His,

which is endless. We weary Him indeed, but we do not weary Him out, with our iniquities. [Our] sin stretches far; but God's patient love overlaps it.[9]

The Solution to Sin

What can we do? If sin is so pervasive, are we responsible? The biblical answer is simply yes, we are. If sin is rebellion, then that rebellion is our responsibility. God offers sinners grace but urges sinners to give up their rebellion. This is where repentance comes in.

It was the great prophets during the monarchical period—Amos, Hosea, Isaiah, and Micah—who led Israel to see that sin is something intensely spiritual and, consequently, deeply tragic. They proclaimed that sin in its awful reality does not involve the violation of a taboo or the transgression of an external ordinance; rather, it touches on our personal standing with God. Repentance was one of their major themes. When the people "turned away from God" (1 Kings 9:6), the prophets called on them to turn back. They said it over and over again: Repent! Turn back! This is clear in Ezekiel 33:11:

> Say to them, As I live, says the Lord GOD, I have no pleasure in the death of the wicked, but that the wicked turn from their ways and live; turn back, turn back from your evil ways; for why will you die, O house of Israel?

We have been taught to feel that guilt is a bad thing. "Don't lay any guilt trips on me!" has become the watchword of the age. But a true spiritual sense of guilt, which includes deep sorrow and shame, follows from the knowledge that sin is a personal affront against a holy and righteous God. The Psalms are full of this kind of realization:

> For my iniquities have gone over my head;
>   they weigh like a burden too heavy for me. . . .
> I am utterly bowed down and prostrate;
>   all day long I go around mourning.
>   (Ps. 38:4, 6)

> For I know my transgressions,
>   and my sin is ever before me.
> Against you, you alone, have I sinned,
>   and done what is evil in your sight,
> so that you are justified in your sentence
>   and blameless when you pass judgment.
>   (51:3–4)

In the Old Testament, the idea of repentance is often expressed by the word *shub*, which means both "turn" and "return." It represents a reorientation of one's whole life and personality. It means forsaking sin and turning back to God's ways of righteousness. This is why the prophets insisted that what the Lord requires is not sacrifice but a "clean heart." The greatest sacrifice we can make is our contrition, our returning to God with renewed commitment.

The New Testament makes it clear that sincere repentance is necessary for entrance into the kingdom of God. John the Baptist echoed the prophets' call to repentance, and Jesus made it the keynote of his Galilean preaching. Repentance is not passive but active. Like the Hebrew word *shub*, the Greek word *metanoia* involves a turning around, a complete change, a turning back to God. It results in a new lifestyle, a reorientation of the personality, a conversion. Many of the parables have to do with repentance, notably those in Luke 15: "The Lost Boy," "The Lost Sheep," and "The Lost Coin."

Acts makes it clear that the preaching of the apostles always included a call to repentance. Peter's sermon in Acts 3:19 includes these words: "Repent therefore, and turn to God so that your sins may be wiped out." In another place, Peter connects repentance and baptism: "Repent, and be baptized every one of you in the name of Jesus Christ so that your sins may be forgiven" (Acts 2:38).

Forgiveness

Forgiveness is a gift of God's grace. It is not based on "what we deserve." We cannot earn it. God acts to take away the obstacles or barriers that separate us, opening the way to reconciliation and a restoration of the covenant relationship. The Hebrew word for forgiveness throws rich light onto this doctrine. It can mean "send away," "cover," "remove," or "wipe away." These vivid metaphors suggest images of a housewife who sweeps away the trash, covers torn clothing with new patches, and removes and wipes away spots and blemishes from clothing and dishes. All is restored to beauty, usefulness, order, and harmony. When we are separated from God by sin, we need forgiveness to make this reconciliation possible. This kind of forgiveness is based not on our achievements but on God's mercy.

The Old Testament sacrifices, properly understood, were a dramatic reenactment of repentance and forgiveness. The individual's approach to the altar indicated an awareness of sin and one's need for forgiveness. Placing hands on the sacrifice was a symbol of identification with the gift. Killing the sacrifice represented the offering up of one's life. Burning a portion of it symbolized its acceptance by God, and the sacrificial meal meant the restoration of fellowship.

This deeper meaning was often lost, however, as sacrifices became routine and perfunctory. Thus, the prophets were compelled to remind the people that forgiveness is not gained by the performance of rituals; it is the free gift of a loving God, who says, "For I will forgive their iniquity, and remember their sin no more" (Jer. 31:34b). Recognition of that great love drives us to our knees in contrition and repentance. The prophets also reminded the people that true repentance is shown by doing justice, loving kindness, and walking humbly with God (Micah 6:8).

The New Testament has the same basic understanding of forgiveness as the Old Testament: the sending away of sins so that reconciliation is possible. However, there is a difference, for in the New Testament, forgiveness is related to the fulfillment of the messianic kingdom. Jesus stressed the necessity of "unlimited forgiveness" as a mark of that kingdom. When Peter asked if there were limits to forgiveness, Jesus responded emphatically that there were none, that we should forgive seventy-seven times. Douglas Hare makes an interesting connection between the way this number is used here and the way it is used in Genesis 4:24, when Lamech boasts that he will avenge himself seventy-sevenfold on anyone who dares attack him. Hare suggests that forgiveness is presented as the antonym of revenge. "Followers of Jesus must renounce the very human intention of getting even with someone who repeatedly injures them. They are called to be Lamech's polar opposite."[10] Jesus illustrated unlimited forgiveness with the parable of the unmerciful servant (Matt. 18:23–35), concluding with the exhortation to "forgive your brother or sister from your heart."

When we respond to Jesus' call to "repent and believe in the gospel," we are not only forgiven but able to forgive others. Recently, I was describing to a friend the unforgiving behavior of an acquaintance, when my friend interrupted to ask, "Is he a Christian?" I was startled and was about to answer, "Of course, he's a member of such and such a church," when I realized that his question had a deeper intent. Can we be followers of Christ and be unforgiving? This is the point Jesus was trying to make to Peter. We are called into a lifestyle of "unlimited forgiveness" by God's forgiveness of us.

Forgiveness means that we are restored to covenant fellowship; that we have become a new creation; that we are reconciled to God through Christ (2 Cor. 5:17–18). The challenge that faces us, then, is how to live every day as those who are forgiven and freed from the burden of sin.

Chapter 5

Righteousness

When kings like Saul, David, and Solomon take the helm of the nation, a new period begins for Israel. Royal sovereigns provide the people with a symbol of unity and stability, but it is short-lived. After Solomon, the kingdom splits apart into Israel in the north and Judah in the south. Israel lasts for nearly two centuries before it is swallowed up by the Assyrian Empire, while Judah survives for another century or so. Because the people suffer so often from poor political and social conditions, various prophets arise to call people to account, reminding them of their responsibility to keep the covenantal promises and to restore righteousness to the land.

A funny thing has happened to religious language in the last two thousand years. We find ourselves uncomfortable with or even embarrassed by some of the terms most frequently used in Scripture to describe people who loved God. As a result, we've simply eliminated them from our everyday speech. One of those terms is *righteous.* How often do you refer to another person as righteous? How often do you apply that adjective to yourself? We have no problem with being called just, fair, honest, or firm, but don't call us righteous!

Why is it that we are so reluctant to claim that attribute? The answer is obvious: we hesitate because it seems presumptuous, because we are too well aware of our feet of clay, because we don't really "feel" righteous, or because we have a horror of being like the Pharisees, whom we think of as "*self*-righteous."

The disappearance of this word from our religious language is a tragic loss. In scriptural usage, "righteousness" is not an unattainable goal, like moral perfection. It is not marked by hypocrisy, as is the term *self-righteous.* It is the mark of faithfulness. In fact, it is one of the distinguishing characteristics of God's children. The Hebrew word for righteousness is *tsedek.* This rich and complex word can mean an astonishing variety of things: straightness, firmness, justice, honesty, faithfulness, piety, mercy, and mildness. It is not coincidental that many of these characteristics are echoed in the Beatitudes of the Sermon on the Mount, for those sayings are a part of Jesus' attempt to reorient God's people to a proper understanding of righteousness. He wanted to call them back to the original meaning of this rich term that had been reduced by many to a sterile ritualism. One was considered righteous if one gave alms, made the proper sacrifices, and observed the rules of the tradition. These rules were described in the *halakah,* the complex oral tradition developed by the rabbis that sought to apply the law to every situation of life. But in the Old Testament, particularly in the teachings of the prophets, righteousness is almost *never* associated with observing ritual. Instead, it is intimately bound up with the practice of justice, compassion, and obedience to the covenant relationship with God. In this session, we look more closely at these three aspects of righteousness, particularly through the eyes of the prophets.

There can be no question about the importance of the concept of righteousness in Scripture. The New Revised Standard Version records 253 uses of the word. It is often paralleled with *justice,* a word that comes from the same root. Many examples of this parallelism are found in Psalms and Proverbs, including these: "[God] loves righteousness and justice" (Ps. 33:5); "To do righteousness and justice is more acceptable to the LORD than sacrifice" (Prov. 21:3).

Although there are many descriptions of righteousness in the Wisdom literature of the Old Testament, it is in the powerful words of the Old Testament prophets that the call to righteousness reaches its peak. It is central to the message of Isaiah, but it is also found in Jeremiah, Ezekiel, Daniel, Hosea, Amos, Zephaniah, and Malachi. One of the best-known calls to righteousness is in Amos: "Let justice roll down like waters, and righteousness like an ever-flowing stream" (Amos 5:24). The sins of the people during the monarchical period provided the necessity for this urgent call on the part of the prophets.

Micah 6:8 contains a succinct summary of three major aspects of biblical righteousness:

> He has told you, O mortal, what is good;
>   and what does the LORD require of you
> but to do justice, and to love kindness,
>   and to walk humbly with your God?

"Doing justice" describes legal righteousness. "Loving kindness" is basic to social righteousness, and "walking humbly with God" is an accurate description of religious righteousness. If we are to truly understand biblical righteousness, it is helpful to take a closer look at these broad and sometimes overlapping categories.

Legal Righteousness: How We Live with Others

The word *tsedek* is frequently translated as "justice," "judgment," or "justification." All of these are legal terms. Do you ever find yourself saying, "It's just not right!" in situations of unfairness or injustice? The voice of legal righteousness speaks out against such unfairness and then decrees patterns of behavior that will correct those situations. In this way, legal righteousness maintains and protects the community, enabling people to live *with* others in safety and security. Without these patterns of justice and fairness, chaos reigns.

In Scripture, legal righteousness guarantees equal rights for all and seeks to restore rights to those from whom they have been taken. Many of the covenant laws were instruments of this kind of righteousness. Exodus 23 provides some clear examples:

> You shall not pervert the justice due to your poor in their lawsuits. Keep far from a false charge, and do not kill the innocent and those in the right, for I will not acquit the guilty. You shall take no bribe, for a bribe blinds the officials, and subverts the cause of those who are in the right. You shall not oppress a resident alien.
>
> (Exod. 23:6–9a)

In Israel's history, both judges and kings had the responsibility of upholding this kind of legal righteousness or justice.

Moses was perhaps the first real judge, but on the advice of his father-in-law Jethro, Moses appointed other judges to assist him in his huge task. They were described as "able men among all the people, men who fear God, are trustworthy, and hate dishonest gain" (Exod. 18:21). During the conquest of Canaan, judges were men and women who were primarily military leaders; they both delivered and governed the people. In the monarchical period, the kings were the supreme judges, although on occasion they appointed regional judges.

The supreme judge and upholder of righteousness and justice in the Old Testament, however, is God. God is the judge who exemplifies the true meaning of legal righteousness, and God is the model for kings and judges. Psalm 7 describes how God operates by playing on the various meanings of *tsedek*:

> The LORD *judges* the peoples;
>> *judge* me, O LORD, according to my *righteousness*
>> and according to the integrity that is in me.
> O let the evil of the wicked come to an end,
>> but establish the *righteous,*
> you who *test* the minds and hearts,
>> O *righteous* God.
> God is my shield,
>> who saves the *upright* in heart.
> God is a *righteous judge,*
>> and a God who has indignation every day.
>>> (Ps. 7:8–11, italics added)

The prophets, however, did not leave the responsibility for legal righteousness in the hands of judges and kings but saw it as the responsibility of all of God's people. Amos challenged Israel to "let justice roll down like waters, and righteousness like an ever-flowing stream" (5:24). Note the dynamic quality of justice in Amos's vocabulary. Justice is not passive. It is not "still waters" but a rushing torrent. Justice is not something we leave to others; justice is something we *do.* It is the active response of God's people to what God has done for them. It means providing justice for the stranger because "you were strangers in the land of Egypt" (Deut. 10:19). Justice requires more than sympathy for the powerless; it means acting as their *advocate.*

When the prophets speak of legal righteousness and justice, they are not speaking philosophically. Instead, their language is vivid; it denounces those who "sell . . . the needy for a pair of sandals" and "trample the head of the poor" (Amos 2:6–7). They address the wealthy women of Samaria, comparing them to fat cows of Bashan (Amos 4:1), and they warn the complacent women taking their ease (Isa. 32:11). They remind the comfortably affluent that they are surrounded with the hungry, homeless poor; with helpless widows, orphans, and strangers; with the powerless and the oppressed. They dare to say that true righteousness is found in ministering justice to these, not in the scrupulous observance of fast days and feast days.

This message was not easy for people to hear two thousand years ago, and it is not easy today. It summons God's people to stir out of their easy chairs, turn off their TV screens, and use their imaginations and energy to find new ways to *do* justice, becoming advocates for the poor and giving voice to the powerless. When that happens, they will begin truly to be God's righteous people.

Social Righteousness: How We Live for Others

In the prophetic mind, however, righteousness went far beyond mere equal rights. It involved "social righteousness" as well, which protected the well-being of the covenant community in another way: through demonstrations of caring and compassion. One of the best demonstrations of this kind of righteousness is that of Job, who "delivered the poor who cried, and the orphan who had no helper," who "caused the widow's heart to sing for joy" and was "eyes to the blind, and feet to the lame." He was also "a father to the needy," and one who "championed the cause of the stranger" (Job 29:12–13, 16).

That's a lot to live up to! If we could just do half as much! Psalm 112 also describes those who understand this form of righteousness:

> They rise in the darkness as a light for the upright;
>> they are gracious, merciful, and righteous.
> It is well with those who deal generously and lend,
>> who conduct their affairs with justice.
> For the righteous will never be moved;
>> they will be remembered forever.
> They are not afraid of evil tidings;
>> their hearts are firm, secure in the LORD.
> Their hearts are steady, they will not be afraid;
>> in the end they will look in triumph on their foes.
> They have distributed freely, they have given to the poor;
>> their righteousness endures forever.
>
> (Ps. 112:4–9)

Isaiah 58 provides one of the most passionate exhortations to social righteousness, along with a ringing indictment of the ritualized religion that had lost its core of compassion:

> Is not this the fast that I choose:
>> to loose the bonds of injustice,
>> to undo the thongs of the yoke,
> to let the oppressed go free,
>> and to break every yoke?
> Is it not to share your bread with the hungry,
>> and bring the homeless poor into your house;
> when you see the naked, to cover them,
>> and not to hide yourself from your own kin?
>
> (Isa. 58:6–7)

Isaiah is making a plea for true righteousness based on the kind of warmth, compassion, and caring that keeps a community together, rather than an empty religiosity based on self-concern. A community that truly cares is a community of stability, solidarity, and *shalom*, where everyone's needs are met: no more injustice, oppression, hunger, homelessness, nakedness. It is the way God's people are supposed to live.

This emphasis on compassion and generosity to the poor resulted in a close association of "righteousness" with almsgiving by Jesus' time. Giving alms was considered by Judaism to be the foremost act of piety, and it was a way to show others how "righteous" one was. Jesus was speaking about public almsgiving when he said, "Beware of practicing your piety before others in order to be seen by them; for then you have no reward from your Father in heaven" (Matt. 6:1).

The importance placed on almsgiving resulted in the "Eight Degrees of Tsedakah (Righteousness)" defined by one of the greatest Hebrew scholars, the twelfth-century Jewish rabbi Maimonides. These still stand as a reminder of what true righteousness is all about. "There are eight degrees in the giving of *tsedakah*," he writes, "one higher than the other":

1. Those who give grudgingly, reluctantly, or with regret.
2. Those who give less than is fitting, but give graciously.
3. Those who give what is fitting, but only after being asked.
4. Those who give before being asked.
5. Those who give without knowing to whom, although the recipients know the identity of the donors.
6. Those who give without making their identity known to the recipients.
7. Those who give without knowing to whom, and neither do the recipients know from whom they receive.
8. Those who help others by giving a gift or loan, or by making them business partners or finding them employment, thereby helping them dispense aid to others. As Scripture says, "You shall strengthen him, be he a stranger or a settler, he shall live with you" (Leviticus 23:35). This means strengthening them in such a manner that falling into want is prevented.[1]

In the Old Testament, the righteous person was identified by concrete acts such as giving liberally to the poor, showing hospitality, and living at peace with neighbors. The outcome of such righteousness is expressed in Isaiah 32:17–18: "The effect of righteousness will be peace, and the result of righteousness, quietness and trust forever. My people will abide in a peaceful habitation, in secure dwellings, and in quiet resting places." What better picture could there be of the *shalom* of the peaceable kingdom? This is the world for which we long in our deepest dreams and for which we continue to pray.

Albert Schweitzer gave the world an example of social righteousness as he practiced medicine in his jungle hospital of Lambarene in the heart of Africa. On one occasion, a badly injured man was brought in for treatment. One of the African attendants protested, "This man is a thief. He was here before and stole drugs and sold them. He has no claim on us again." Schweitzer's eyes flashed. "What would Jesus have answered when someone came to Him in pain? Waste no time; get him to the operating room!" Schweitzer believed that though we all must work to live, our real purpose in life is to show compassion in helping others. Only then, he emphasized, do we become true human beings. "So many people come here to Lambarene," he said, "and others wish to but are unable to come. But everyone is capable of his own Lambarene."[2] By the biblical definitions we have been examining, Schweitzer was, indeed, a righteous man.

The movie *Schindler's List* portrayed a German Nazi, who gave his fortune to free his Jewish employees from the death camps. He was immortalized in Israel on the "Avenue of Righteous Gentiles." Toward the end of the movie, Schindler uttered the poignant comment "I could have done so much more." That passionate commitment is the hallmark of a person who practices social righteousness.

Religious Righteousness: How We Live for God

In addition to legal and social righteousness, the Old Testament recognizes what may be termed religious righteousness. In essence, this righteousness was expressed by obedience to the commands of the covenant. This obedience is not an effort to merit God's grace by one's righteousness but is, instead, a response to that grace in the way life is lived. It is rooted in God's righteousness, which Isaiah describes in this way:

> I am the LORD, I have called you in righteousness,
>   I have taken you by the hand and kept you;
> I have given you as a covenant to the people,
>   a light to the nations,
>   to open the eyes that are blind,
> to bring out the prisoners from the dungeon,
>   from the prison those who sit in darkness.
> (Isa. 42:6–7)

The Old Testament makes it clear that God established the covenant relationship for the well-being of the community of God's people. Within this covenant
relationship of grace, the law provides a guide to righteous living. Its seemingly impossible demands have one purpose: to make Israel holy. The righteous are those who live in obedience to the covenant by respecting the laws
that uphold and maintain the covenant community. These laws form the
basis for *legal righteousness* by insuring the practice of justice, just as they
form the basis for *social righteousness* by insuring the practice of compassion.

All these laws, however, have their roots in *religious righteousness*, which
involves recognition of the covenant relationship. All righteousness is given
definition by the character of God, the truly righteous judge described in
Deuteronomy 10:17b–18 as one "who is not partial and takes no bribe, who
executes justice for the orphan and the widow, and who loves the strangers,
providing them food and clothing." God's righteousness is demonstrated
throughout Scripture in powerful acts that preserve and protect and restore the
community.

The eighth-century prophets (Amos, Hosea, Isaiah, and Micah) increas-
ingly connected the idea of righteousness with salvation and redemption. Isaiah refers to God as "a righteous God and Savior" (Isa. 45:21) because God's
righteous judgments are seen as saving judgments. Through these saving acts,
God fulfills the demands of the covenant relationship. "The Holy God shows
himself holy by righteousness" (Isa. 5:16). Nevertheless, the righteousness of
God's people is not as steadfast as God's: "the righteous turn away from their
righteousness" (Ezek. 18:26). God laments: "O that you had paid attention to
my commandments! Then your prosperity would have been like a river, and
your success like the waves of the sea" (Isa. 48:18). Stubborn and stiff-necked,
God's people keep refusing to turn to God in faith; they do not practice justice or compassion. Their righteousness hangs in shreds.

It is at this point that Isaiah speaks words of great hope and comfort. In
spite of the people's unrighteousness, God will not forsake them. "I have chosen you and not cast you off; do not fear, for I am with you" (Isa. 41:9). In
spite of the people's unrighteousness, the covenant stands. "My steadfast love
shall not depart from you, and my covenant of peace shall not be removed,
says the LORD, who has compassion on you" (54:10). God will intervene on
behalf of the undeserving people, will deliver them, forgive them, and declare
them to be all right, justified, made righteous. "In righteousness you shall be
established" (54:14). It is up to the people to accept this deliverance and
claim the righteousness that God has provided for them. The ultimate understanding of this gift of grace comes through the New Testament message of

salvation through Jesus Christ. "While we still were sinners Christ died for us" (Rom. 5:8).

Righteousness in the New Testament

In the New Testament, righteousness is also expressed in the same three categories: legal, social, and religious. The least amount of attention is given to legal righteousness, although Paul borrowed its legal language to lay a foundation for a new understanding of grace. God, as the supreme judge, justifies the unjustifiable by judicial decree. "They are now justified by his grace as a gift" (Rom. 3:24). In Hebrews, there is a reference to God's justice in the sense of fairness: "For God is not unjust; he will not overlook your work and the love that you showed for his sake in serving the saints, as you still do" (Heb. 6:10).

Social righteousness, particularly in relationships within the covenant community, is clearly an important part of Jesus' teachings. In the Sermon on the Mount, righteousness and compassion are inseparable. Jesus describes several unrighteous acts that have the capacity to destroy the community by making compassionate relationships impossible: revenge, lust, even hatred of enemies.

The kind of righteousness for which Jesus called goes beyond the narrow legalism of the Pharisees. It put compassion above scrupulous obedience of the "jots and tittles" of the Law. Jesus charged the Pharisees with performing ritual acts of "righteousness" (such as almsgiving) from selfish motives. He taught that as God had acted in righteousness, fulfilling the covenant relationship by showing forgiving love to us, so we must act in righteousness, fulfilling the demands of the covenant by showing love toward others.

The New Testament sees religious righteousness as the prophets did: accepting the covenant relationship with God with repentance, faith, and obedience. Righteousness depends on God. It is God who initiates the covenant relationship; it is God who makes us righteous. In this category, there is no true righteousness apart from a relationship with God. A model of this kind of righteousness was Simeon; since he was "righteous and devout, looking forward to the consolation of Israel, and the Holy Spirit rested on him" (Luke 2:25).

But even though the Sermon on the Mount is about true righteousness, it is Paul, not Jesus, who uses the word *righteousness* the most. When the apostle writes about the law of righteousness in Romans 9:31, he is referring to the ethical demands of the Mosaic Law, but when he uses the phrase "the righteousness of God," he is referring to the salvation that God accomplishes through Christ. In Romans 10:10, Paul writes, "For one believes with the heart and so is justified, and one confesses with the mouth and so is saved." The Greek word for righteousness, *dikaiosune,* can also be translated "justification." In both the Old and New Testaments, to be justified means to be brought into right relations with another. We can achieve this with other human beings, but there is nothing we can do to secure our justification before God. As the psalmist said, "No one living is righteous before you" (Ps. 143:2). We can continue in and maintain our relationship with God by obedience and devotion, but the establishment of that relationship is the gift of grace. We are justified (that is, made righteous) by grace and grace alone.

Paul teaches that religious righteousness precedes both social and legal righteousness. Grace comes first, followed by faith, an attitude of gratitude and receptivity to God's grace, then by compassion and justice. In his book *Christian Doctrine,* Shirley Guthrie asks at the beginning of the chapter on justification:

> Are you a Christian? If you believe in Christ, then why are you so impatient with your children? Why do you talk about other people behind their backs? Do you pay your employees a fair wage? What are you doing to obey Jesus' command to minister to the poor, the oppressed, the imprisoned?[3]

At the end of the chapter, he returns to the same question:

> According to the doctrine of justification, Christians are those who know that they are guilty of offending God and of hurting other people and themselves by their attempts to justify themselves. They are those who believe that *nevertheless*, despite everything, they are forgiven, loved and accepted by God's grace in Jesus Christ. And as they experience freedom from the anxious or proud need to justify themselves, they also experience a new freedom for God and other people and a new freedom to accept and be themselves.[4]

Chapter 6

Hope

The time of the kings ends disastrously as Judah, too, is destroyed. The Babylonian Empire desecrates the Temple, burns the city of Jerusalem, and carries many of the people of Judah into captivity. Despair descends on the downtrodden people. The future seems bleak, as God's unconditional covenant appears to have collapsed. Those who remain in the land live in poverty and gloom. Those who have been carried to Babylon think that their homes have been lost forever. Living through such pain and disaster, the people are forced to learn the meaning of a deep and abiding hope, hope that can resist trouble and overcome seemingly overwhelming evil.

We probably cannot hope to feel fully the shock that the exile must have created in the souls of believing Israelites. Remember that this is the people who had received the covenant we spoke of earlier. The promise that they would be God's special people went as far back as Abraham. They remembered that the promise had been assured at Mount Sinai and a land had been given to them as their habitation. They recalled that, according to authoritative prophetic words, their royal line would last through all generations. To top it all off, they experienced God's continuing presence in the Temple in the holy city of Jerusalem.

What feelings must have swirled in their hearts when they realized that the prophecies of destruction by the prophet Jeremiah were coming true? For indeed, the armies of the foreign king, Nebuchadnezzar, broke down Jerusalem piece by piece, burned the city with fire, and carried many of its inhabitants away to far-off Babylon. We can get some sense of how the people of Israel must have felt if we read a few verses from Psalm 137:1–4:

By the rivers of Babylon—
    there we sat down and there we wept
    when we remembered Zion.
On the willows there
    we hung up our harps.
For there our captors
    asked us for songs,
and our tormentors asked for mirth, saying,
    "Sing us one of the songs of Zion!"
How could we sing the LORD's song
    in a foreign land?

This psalm offers a lament for an appalling development in Israel's national life. You might wonder why we have begun with such a depressing passage. After all, the theme of this chapter is *hope*.

Here is the reason for starting with lamentations: the Bible does not offer us hope purely and simply at times when things in our life have been going well, when our mood is optimistic, and when the future looks bright. Rather, hope goes much deeper than that. Oftentimes, we have to go through lament to get to hope. To understand this paradoxical reality, we will need to look closely at the depths of despair into which Israel was hurled during this disturbing, depressing time of exile.

A Nation in Torment

An entire book in the Old Testament is devoted to the disaster of the captivity and resulting exile. That book is Lamentations. Traditionally, the book has been associated with Jeremiah, and some versions of the Bible title it the Lamentations of Jeremiah. However, we do not really know who wrote the book. Today, while some people speculate about the identity of the author of this short writing, most are content to say that the author is anonymous.

Whoever the author of Lamentations was, he writes as a representative of the people of Judah, and he provides us with a heart-wrenching account of the despair that settled over many who experienced this frightful event in Israel's history. Listen to some of the words of distress in the first chapter of the writing:

How lonely sits the city
    that once was full of people!
How like a widow she has become,
    she that was great among the nations! . . .

Judah has gone into exile with suffering
   and hard servitude;
she lives now among the nations,
   and finds no resting place; . . .
Jerusalem remembers,
   in the days of her affliction and wandering,
all the precious things
   that were hers in days of old.
(Lam. 1:1, 3, 7)

It's a sad scene, isn't it? A sense of loss, a feeling of despair, an ache of lone-liness: all these well up from the depths of broken hearts.

Is it nothing to you, all you who pass by?
   Look and see
if there is any sorrow like my sorrow. . . .
For these things I weep;
   my eyes flow with tears;
for a comforter is far from me.
(Lam. 1:12, 16)

Now let's get more specific. The suffering of nations is really about the affliction of people—concrete, living and breathing individual women and men who undergo intense pain and affliction. The writer of Lamentations, who has spoken for the nation in chapter 1, writes about his own torment in chapter 3:

I am one who has seen affliction
   under the rod of God's wrath;
he has driven and brought me
   into darkness without any light. . . .
He has made my flesh and my skin waste away,
   and broken my bones; . . .
though I call and cry for help,
   he shuts out my prayer. . . .
He has made my teeth grind on gravel,
   and made me cower in ashes;
my soul is bereft of peace;
   I have forgotten what happiness is;
so I say, "Gone is my glory,
   and all that I had hoped for from the LORD."
(Lam. 3:1–2, 4, 8, 16–18)

The sorrow and the distress have become personal as the writer describes his anguish in graphic terms. If you read the entire chapter, you may say "almost too graphically."

Do you hear how the writer is gasping for faith here? "Can I still trust in the Lord?" he is asking. "Why does a supposedly good God permit so much suffering, rejection, and pain? Is it possible to believe in God at all?" These are not just questions for the biblical writers. Whenever major, highly publicized events occur, these questions always spring to the surface. Planes fall from the sky. People are paralyzed in freak accidents. Dictators enrich themselves while their people starve. Madmen shoot strangers in the streets. Sometimes children shoot other children.

There is a lot of pain and grief in this world. It isn't just shocking events or highly publicized tragedies that cause distress. Personal problems may also create distress: a job loss or a poor investment or a broken marriage; a child in trouble, an unexpected illness, or the death of a beloved grandparent. Any of these events, and many more besides, can cause pain and anguish.

If you have ever read any mountain-climbing stories, you will know that one of the greatest dangers faced by climbers is altitude sickness. It begins to rip at the lungs, and it causes intense pain, even anguish, in every corner of your body. Its effects can ravage even a healthy, well-trained physique.[1] Altitude sickness provides a pointed image for the effects that upsetting, disturbing events can have on us. Such troubles can rip at our heart and cause pain and nausea through our whole being. They leave us gasping for air.

There are many reasons for lament. Sometimes people suggest that the thing to do when you face adversity or experience an anguishing situation is to follow the advice of the old phrase "Keep a stiff upper lip." Suppress the pain. Overlook the suffering. Don't let tears come to your eyes. Luckily, that's not the approach taken by Lamentations or by other laments in the Scriptures. Instead, the biblical writers acknowledge pain. They admit to suffering. They allow the experience of anguish and desolation and torment to stand squarely in the center for all to see. Biblical writers say in so many words: "You can be honest with God. You can share your true feelings with those around you."

That's good for us to remember. Many of us are not very good at lamenting. In response to the question "How are you?" we are taught from early years to offer a smile and say, "I'm fine," while quickly moving to another topic. But we're not always fine, and we're not always smiling inside. Even in funeral homes, many of us often don't cry very much, if at all. For some reason, we seem to be uncomfortable talking about our own losses and our own deep sadness. Yet we also know, as this book of Lamentations makes abundantly clear, that some things in life do cause heartache. Some events do bring about intense inner pain and suffering. Our best advice, therefore, is to accept the pain and to face the grief head on. When something in life causes hurt, when something important is broken, then practice lamenting. Speak with God about your anguish. Pour out your heart about the pain. Describe how awful it feels. Cry out, "Why, O Lord?" And ask for help, and hope, and faith.

A Time of Astonishment

If anything is unpredictable, it is what may happen in world history. Just think back a few years now to the totally unexpected collapse of communism. The symbolic destruction of the Berlin wall was coupled with a turn to democracy in Eastern Europe that quickly changed the landscape there and realigned many of the power blocs among the nations of the world. Something just as surprising, and just as revolutionary, occurred when the new king of the Persian Empire adopted a revised policy toward his subject peoples. In the first year of his reign, Cyrus made decrees like this one recorded in the Hebrew Scriptures:

> Thus says King Cyrus of Persia: the LORD, the God of heaven, has given me all the kingdoms of the earth, and he has charged me to build him a house at Jerusalem in Judah. Any of those among you who are of his people—may their God be with them!—are now permitted to go up to Jerusalem in Judah, and rebuild the house of the LORD, the God of Israel.
>
> (Ezra 1:2–3)

We can presume that the writers have embellished Cyrus's respect for Israel's God. He seems to have made similar edicts regarding a variety of peoples who had been transported by force from their homelands to other, foreign nations. Be that as it may, the effect of Cyrus's astonishing decrees was to reverse a long-standing policy of deportation. The unexpected had truly come about: displaced, disinherited peoples were now permitted to return to their homelands. They could worship once again in their own traditional religious style on their own native soil. They could govern their own affairs with a degree of self-control, as a province within the greater empire.

Thus it was that what had appeared to be the absolute destruction of the people and the faith of Israel came full circle. In successive waves, the captives returned to lead in rebuilding their homes. Eventually, they restored the Temple and they rebuilt the walls of the city. You can sense the amazement, the joy, and the disbelief that the people felt as you read the words of Psalm 126:1–2:

> When the LORD restored the fortunes of Zion,
>   we were like those who dream.
> Then our mouth was filled with laughter,
>   And our tongue with shouts of joy.

A brief footnote is in order: You may know that not everything was wondrous once the people returned to the land. In fact, when given the opportunity to return to Jerusalem, most people preferred to remain in Babylon.

Those who did return found that it was hard to eke out a living. The earlier glory of the kingdoms, especially the splendor that had existed under David and Solomon, never materialized. The people of Judah continued to be a subject nation, living in a rather insignificant land and struggling to make ends meet. They practiced their faith at a shrine that could in no way rival the beauty of Solomon's temple, and they hung on more and more fiercely to a lifestyle of ritual and practices that set them farther and farther apart from the surrounding world.

This postexilic period—or the "time between the testaments," as it is sometimes called—is not the brightest period in Israel's history. Nevertheless, the nation had been restored, and what had appeared, literally, to be a hope-*less* situation had turned around. That is why we can focus on "hope" as our key theme for this period. We can even stay with Lamentations to do that.

A Statement of Hope

The very title Lamentations implies that there isn't going to be much that is cheery or optimistic in this book. Yet, nestled in the midst of the sadness and the gloom that permeate the writing, there is also something else. It is positive. It is optimistic. It is hopeful. It is this:

> The steadfast love of the LORD never ceases,
>   his mercies never come to an end;
> they are new every morning;
>   great is your faithfulness. . . .
> The LORD is good to those who wait for him,
>   to the soul that seeks him.
> It is good that one should wait quietly
>   for the salvation of the LORD.
>   (Lam. 3:22–23, 25–26)

Would you have anticipated finding these words in a book called Lamentations? This is one of the most beautiful passages in the whole of the Scriptures. It sparkles like a diamond in a costly setting. Yet the setting for this gemstone is a distressing lamentation. "The steadfast love of the LORD never ceases, [God's] mercies never come to an end." No wonder these words provided the inspiration for a popular hymn, "Great Is Thy Faithfulness."

You might conclude that, if God can bring about something so astounding as the restoration of Israel, then anything is possible. Not surprisingly, that is really the underlying lesson the Scriptures mean for us to learn, though it seems to take most of us a long time to master it. Think of the words the angel Gabriel uses in announcing to Mary the amazing news that her relative Elizabeth is expecting her first child in her old age. Gabriel declares in a matter-of-fact tone, "For nothing will be impossible with God" (Luke 1:37).

Even beyond Elizabeth's incredible miracle, however, more is possible: the incarnation of Jesus Christ, for example. And then there is the miracle of Easter: the resurrection of Jesus Christ as well! No wonder the writer of Lamentations can proclaim that it is "good that one should wait quietly for the salvation of the LORD." In a novel by Pat Conroy, titled *Beach Music*, the lead character in the story, Jack, is sitting with his mother, Lucy, who has reached the endstage of cancer. As she warns her son how short her remaining time is, he asks, "Does believing in God help any?" Lucy's resolute reply is this: "Believe me when I tell you it's the only thing that helps at all."[2]

Hope is for times when the future looks bleak. It is for times when things are going against us, and when our dreams and desires have been shattered. Hope is for those moments when it seems that the fabric of our lives has been ripped and torn beyond repair. You may have experienced such times in your own life, perhaps more than once. If so, you may also have learned that those are especially the times to hang for dear life onto words like the ones in Lamentations: "The steadfast love of the LORD never ceases, God's mercies never come to an end; they are new every morning."

If we are going through a trying period of pain and distress, there is only one way to conquer it: by waiting. You may not have noticed the last verse in our earlier quotation from Lamentations: "It is good that one should wait quietly for the salvation of the LORD." Waiting is hard work. It tries our patience. It forces us to live with pain and distress. Sometimes the heavy weight of heartache feels like it will overwhelm us entirely. Waiting is not something we generally like to do very much, especially in a culture that cries out to us to get everything and anything we want *now*—if not sooner.

Yet "waiting" has a good pedigree in the Scriptures. The prophets of Israel encouraged the people often enough to wait. Speaking about a coming vision, for instance, Habakkuk writes, "If it seems to tarry, wait for it; it will surely come, it will not delay" (Hab. 2:3). Another psalmist declares, "I wait for the

LORD, my soul waits, and in his word I hope" (Ps. 130:5). Much earlier in Israel's history, Saul is rejected as king due to his unwillingness to wait for Samuel to come before offering sacrifices (1 Sam. 13:5–15). And much later, near the end of the New Testament, the letter of Second Peter encourages readers to wait for "the coming of the day of God" (2 Peter 3:12). Even the disciples must be told, following the resurrection, that they are "not to leave Jerusalem, but to wait there for the promise" of the Holy Spirit (Acts 1:4).

There seems to be something salutary in waiting. Often, it is not comfortable for us, and sometimes it may nearly overwhelm our spirits. Nevertheless, the patience and contentment that periods of waiting require seem to clear space for faith to grow. Perhaps the waiting period allows time for God to work in our hearts, for a change to come about, for an insight to germinate, for an emotional or spiritual problem to be addressed. Such a period of waiting is not empty and wasted but full of growth and new life. It may equip us with a much richer and fuller spirit, and far greater joy, than we possessed previously.

Our Ultimate Hope

We can still take one more step with this theme. So far, we have been dealing with disturbing realities in this world. We have talked about both the need for and the possibility of holding out in hope under what can sometimes be staggering circumstances. In the New Testament, however, hope is connected most profoundly to future salvation. We could demonstrate this easily, for instance, from a number of the Pauline letters or the letter to the Hebrews (especially chap. 11, which is famous for its focus on hope). Here let's look at the letter of First Peter. Listen to these words from the first chapter:

> Blessed be the God and Father of our Lord Jesus Christ! By his great mercy he has given us a new birth into a living hope through the resurrection of Jesus Christ from the dead, and into an inheritance that is imperishable, undefiled, and unfading, kept in heaven for you.
>
> (1 Peter 1:3–4)

These are the first words after the greeting in this letter. Notice how the writer proclaims that our new birth through Christ's resurrection is a "living hope." Then he identifies this hope with an inheritance that is "imperishable, undefiled, and unfading." As you undoubtedly know, inheritances can be problematic. Plenty of family squabbles have been occasioned by dividing up an inheritance. Sometimes the disputes have resulted in long-term hostilities. If anything, an inheritance carried even more significance in biblical times. That is precisely why First Peter compares our future hope to an inheritance that cannot be defiled. It will not fade or perish. It will not become tarnished, and it is everlasting.

If we take an inventory of our possessions, we will probably not find many—or any—that have this degree of permanence. The flowers of the field perish. Stock markets go up and down. A generation comes and a generation goes. Autos, electronic equipment, and sturdy buildings all fall victim to wear and tear. And so do we. Nothing in this world is secure. This is hard for us to grasp in a culture that seeks to minimize every conceivable risk. Recall all the ways in which we protect ourselves: using triple antibiotic cream on simple cuts, taking vitamin pills by the truckload, teaching children to fear strangers, washing hands with antibacterial soap, buying insurance of all kinds, and on and on. But we cannot secure ourselves against everything. And even if we could eliminate that one certainty—taxes—the other will eventually get us: death.

Yet we do have something that is imperishable: our promised eternal hope. As the Lord asked the prophet Ezekiel about the people of Israel in ancient times: "Can these bones live?" (Ezek. 37:3). The answer from First Peter is that we can and we do live on, because of the living hope that has been set aside for us in the heavens.

Now we should not miss the fact that this hope-filled inheritance is linked to the resurrection of Jesus Christ. In the *Institutes of the Christian Religion*, John Calvin comments that "Christ rose again that he might have us as companions in the life to come."[3] Because Jesus has gone through "the valley of the shadow of death" (Ps. 23: 4, KJV) and returned from the grave, we can be certain that we will be with him in eternity. Easter Sunday proves that, in the language of First Peter, our inheritance is assured. All the darkness and despair in this world culminated in a cross on a hill outside Jerusalem, but the morning light of Easter has triumphed. The amazing affirmation "He is risen!" encapsulates all our hope of a liberation from the bonds of sin and frailty, all our certainty that we are destined not for decay in a tomb but an eternity of peace and goodness and joy without end.

Isn't this what First Peter means in saying that we have "an inheritance kept in heaven for us"? Because we have faith in the resurrection of Jesus Christ, our future—even when we pass through the valley of the shadow of death—is secure in God's promises. Not only that, but we can have hope for those whom we love as well. If you have ever stood by a grave, you know what it is like to long for a friend, a parent, a husband or wife, or perhaps even a child. If so, then you know what it is like to mourn for a lost loved one, and perhaps to edge ever so close to hopelessness.

For some of us, this is where these words about hope and an inheritance can penetrate most deeply into our spirits. The promised hope is not just for us but also for those with whom we have shared life in our own small circle on this earth. For them, too, there is a promised inheritance through Jesus' resurrection. And thus, our inheritance also promises a reunion of sorts: a time when we will be not only united with Christ but reunited with friends and family. This is the deepest sense in which the Scriptures speak of hope.

Chapter 7

Compassion

Within seventy years of the exile to Babylon, God brings the people back to Judah. The city and Temple are rebuilt, and the Law is restored. God's covenant continues intact, although conditions are difficult and a succession of foreign empires rule the Jews, culminating with the Roman occupation of the land. By the time of Jesus, synagogues provide the regular place of worship and teaching; the Pharisees and other groups have become influential; and the law has been extended further and further into daily life. By his own teachings and actions, Jesus seeks to lift people out from under the yoke of a legal righteousness, proclaiming instead a righteousness based on mercy and compassion.

Our God is a God of compassion. The Old Testament bears witness to that great truth, but it is the Gospels that show us its full depth. "For God so loved the world that he gave his only Son" (John 3:16). Jesus gave visible form to God's compassion by being a Messiah of deed as well as of word, a Messiah who restored suffering people to health and well-being, a Messiah who was willing to suffer and die for others. The Gospels portray him as one who fulfilled the words of Isaiah's Servant Song: "Surely he has borne our infirmities and carried our diseases" (Isa. 53:4). Moreover, Jesus called his disciples to lives of compassionate love.

We are far more comfortable with the word *compassion* than we are with *righteousness*. It slips with ease into our daily conversations. "Have a little compassion," we say to the antique dealer, "can't you come down a little on the price of that mirror?" Politicians and public figures love the word. In a recent political campaign, "compassionate conservatism" was an important plank in a candidate's platform. But what does *compassion* really mean? Is biblical compassion different from that championed by politicians and secular altruistic groups? How is it related to those other important biblical words, *pity* and *mercy*? Just what did Jesus do to show compassion? What does his life tell us about the practice of compassion in our own lives?

The Language of Compassion

First of all, note that the words for "compassion," "pity," and "mercy" in the original languages of the Bible are completely interchangeable. There is no clear distinction among them in Greek or Hebrew, and biblical interpreters are left free to choose the word that seems to fit the situation the best. That is why in the Jerusalem Bible's version of Matthew 14:14, Jesus "took pity" on the crowd before feeding them with five loaves and two fish, and in the NRSV, he "had compassion" for them. In Deuteronomy 13:17, the King James Version uses the expression "that the LORD may . . . shew thee mercy," while the NRSV reads "that the LORD may . . . show you compassion."

The most frequently used Hebrew noun for "pity," "mercy," or "compassion" is *rachamim*. Far from being trite or condescending, this is one of the richest words in our theological vocabulary. It can denote an inner feeling of sympathy or love expressed outwardly in helping action; it can mean the tender affection of a parent for a child; or it can mean forgiveness. Most of the time, however, *rachamim* refers to God's love, manifested in saving acts of grace toward the covenant people. The related terms *merciful* and *gracious* are repeatedly used in the Hebrew Scriptures but are *only* used for the Creator and never for the creatures. The frequent use of these words reminds us that the God of the Old Testament is a God of *grace*. The following verses describe that grace:

> The LORD is merciful and gracious,
>   slow to anger and abounding in steadfast love.
> (Ps. 103:8)

> Therefore the LORD waits to be gracious to you;
>   therefore he will rise up to show mercy to you.
> For the LORD is a God of justice;
>   blessed are all those who wait for him.
> (Isa. 30:18)

Rachamim is the plural form of the word *rechem,* which can mean both "guts" and "womb." Old Testament scholar Phyllis Trible has explored this metaphor extensively in her work *God and the Rhetoric of Sexuality*. She describes how appropriate this metaphorical way of speaking of compassion is:

> The womb protects and nourishes but does not possess and control. It yields its treasure in order that wholeness and well-being may happen. Truly it is the way of compassion.[1]

Even though the metaphor of the womb assures us that God's love and compassion for us are like that of a mother for her child, we must not sentimentalize this idea into a kind of mushiness. We must bear in mind that, in the Hebrew Scriptures, God's love is a part of the covenant relationship with the chosen people. It is integrally related to God's faithfulness and characterizes the way God upholds that covenant. God's mercy, God's tender compassion, God's pity, God's "womb love"—like God's steadfast love—are "from everlasting to everlasting" (Ps. 103:17).

In the New Testament, several Greek words are used to express the concept of compassion. The verb used by the sick and poor when they appeal to Jesus for help is *eleeo*, "to show mercy." The two blind men in Matthew 9:27 called out to Jesus, "Have mercy on us (*eleison emas*)." This is the same prayer we sing in the *Kyrie eleison*. This phrase means literally "Lord, help me."

However, a much stronger Greek word is used to express Jesus' reactions to people in need, the almost unpronounceable word *splagchna*. It refers to a person's inner parts: the heart, the liver, the bowels, or the womb. In this way, it is similar to the Hebrew word *rachamim*. *Splagchna* was used in Greek literature in the way we use the word *heart*: as the center of passionate emotions and personal feelings. It literally meant a "gut-churning" reaction—not a passive and distant reaction, but an inner, agitated reaction of mercy (Luke 6:36; Matt. 5:7).

Although there are many stories of Jesus' acts of compassion, there are only a few places in the Gospels where the word *splagchna* is used to describe those acts. Several of these references refer to the stories of Jesus' feeding the crowds who had followed him. Matthew and Mark tell us that he had compassion on the crowds who were "like sheep without a shepherd" (Matt. 9:36; Mark 6:34). On another occasion, Jesus had compassion for the crowds who had followed him, so he "cured their sick" before feeding more than five thousand of them with five loaves and two fish (Matt. 14:14). Mark telescopes these two incidents into one, adding that Jesus' compassion inspired him to "teach them many things" (Mark 6:34).

Jesus had compassion on the crowds because they were hungry after following him for three days (Matt. 15:32; Mark 8:2). The statement that the crowds were "harassed and helpless" like sheep without a shepherd is similar to many Old Testament references that describe God's people as a flock neglected by its shepherds. In Matthew, Jesus uses this occasion to present himself as the promised "good shepherd" and to point out the need for other compassionate shepherds who will work for the "Lord of the harvest."

Luke uses the word *splagchna* to describe Jesus' emotion when he encountered the widow who had lost her only son (Luke 7:11–17). This story is a vivid illustration of Jesus' ministry of compassion. His attention is on the tragic figure of the mother. His heart went out to her in gut-wrenching compassion when he witnessed her grief. He spoke directly to her with words of sympathy and consolation. He defied the laws of ritual cleanliness by touching the funeral bier of the dead son. Finally, he lifted the son into his mother's eager arms. His feeling of compassion was followed first by words of compassion, then by deeds of compassion. Not only did he raise the boy from the dead; the very act of returning the son to the mother revealed Jesus' compassionate pity for those who suffer not only grief but public scorn as well. In those days, the community would have despised the boy's mother, for it was believed that misfortune was the result of sin. Jesus' act was a beautiful testimony to compassion that is free of judging.

The compassion of Jesus was neither sentimental nor superficial. It was a gut-wrenching emotion that moved him to reach out and actively to help others. We often overlook the fact that our English word *compassion* comes from two Latin words, *com* (with) and *passio* (suffering). Compassion means "to suffer with." The essence of God is God's *com-passio*, God's willingness to suffer with us when we suffer. God's "womb love" is suffering love. Jesus' gut-wrenching love for the people is suffering love. It is not based on the worthiness of the people. Were there rascals and freeloaders in the crowds Jesus fed? Probably. His compassion was based on a commitment to the well-being of the other. God's compassion is based on God's steadfast love, God's commitment to our well-being. As Christ's disciples, we are called to display that same sort of commitment to others, to let our guts churn on their behalf, to suffer with and for them.

There is a beautiful contemporary illustration of this kind of commitment to compassion in the book, later to become an Oscar-winning movie, *A Beautiful Mind: The Life of Mathematical Genius and Nobel Laureate John Nash*. Nash suffered from paranoid schizophrenia. Finding him impossible to live with, his wife, Alicia, won a divorce. However, after forty years of separation, she came back to him with a renewed commitment and a willingness to suffer for his well-being.

Alicia was a proud woman, always sensitive to appearances; her loyalty and compassion outweighed her concern for what others might think. She was patient. She bit her tongue. She made very few demands on Nash. Looking back, her gentle manner probably played a substantial role in his recovery. . . . Alicia is a scrupulously honest person. She says of the role she has played in protecting Nash simply, "Sometimes you don't plan things. They just turn out that way." She does see that it helped him, though, saying, "Did the way he was treated help him get better? Oh, I think so. He had his room and board, his basic needs taken care of, and not too much pressure. That's what you need: being taken care of and not too much pressure."[2]

The emphasis in Leviticus 19:18 on loving neighbors was not so much on emotional attachment as on the obligation to show compassion toward others by working for their well-being. Such caring is offered without expectation of success or reward. Henri Nouwen said, "Compassion means to lay a bridge over to the other without knowing whether he wants to be reached."[3] Jesus' extraordinary words in the Sermon on the Mount push the envelope on this kind of compassion to an extent that no other rabbi had dared to do. He urged compassionate commitment even toward enemies. "Love your enemies and pray for those who persecute you" (Matt. 5:44). This means not seeking revenge, no more "eye for eye and tooth for tooth," no more wishing the enemy were dead. Instead, it means seeking the welfare even of those who are seeking to do you harm. What does this say to us about the rapidly growing tendency to sue others for malpractice or personal injury? What does it say about our tendency to seek military solutions to world peace? The practice of compassion is difficult and demanding.

Old Testament Foundations for Compassion

It is only in the light of the Old Testament understanding of compassion that we can begin to understand what Jesus taught about it. Such verses as "Blessed are the merciful, for they will receive mercy" (Matt. 5:7) take on a much deeper meaning in the light of the Old Testament.

On the few occasions in the Old Testament when mercy is used as a characteristic of human beings, it is in relational situations, particularly those showing mercy or compassion to the poor. These acts of compassion were seen as homage given to God. To truly love God, one must also love one's neighbor. When Jesus was asked to name the first and greatest commandment, he quoted the well-known Shema: "You shall love the LORD your God with all your heart, and with all your soul, and with all your might" (Deut. 6:5). Then he added these words from Leviticus: "You shall love your neighbor as yourself" (Lev. 19:18). He also expressed this idea of compassion when he said, "Just as you did it to one of the least of these who are members of my family, you did it to me" (Matt. 25:40).

Under the covenant law, there were certain relationships in which mercy and compassion were clearly expected. First was *the family circle*. Compassion, help, love, and consideration among family members were not only expected but required. A lack of compassion meant the destruction of family ties. God criticized Edom, who "pursued his brother with the sword and cast off all pity; he maintained his anger perpetually, and kept his wrath forever" (Amos 1:11).

The levirate laws, which required a man to take on the support of his brother's widow, were provided as instruments of exercising compassion for unfortunate family members (Deut. 25:5–10). Boaz honored this law of compassion by taking responsibility for Ruth's well-being as her next of kin. Behind these laws lay the understanding that God works through human acts of compassion to bring about *shalom* in the world. This is why acts of compassion are ways to honor God and God's intentions. The Good News Bible translates Isaiah's great call to compassion in this way: "Share your food with the hungry and open your homes to the homeless poor. Give clothes to those who have nothing to wear, and do not refuse to help your own relatives" (Isa. 58:7). Isaiah is claiming that such acts of compassion and worship are inseparable. Acts of loving-kindness honor God more than fasting and sacrifices.

Second was *the tribe or community*. One of Job's most poignant pleas is his cry "You are my friends! Take pity on me! The hand of God has struck me down!" (Job 19:21, TEV). Job feels deserted not only by family but also by his entire community of friends. They look at him with disgust; those he loved have turned against him (Job 19:13–14, 19). Love, support, and compassion have been denied him. He cries out to his friends to give him the compassion normally expected of the community, but which he no longer receives.

Finally were *the dependent and the helpless*. Laced throughout the covenant are laws requiring particular compassion for the helpless: widows, orphans, the aged, the poor, and aliens. The gleaning laws cited in Deuteronomy 24:20–21 were exercises in compassion. Over and over again in wisdom literature, particularly in Psalms and Proverbs, we find calls to compassion such as this one: "If you close your ear to the cry of the poor, you will cry out and not be heard" (Prov. 21:13). The prophets bore down on the theme of compassion. Over and over again, they reminded God's people of their covenant responsibility to "show mercy and kindness to one another; do not oppress the widow, the orphan, the alien, or the poor; and do not devise evil in your hearts against one another" (Zech. 7:9). Even royalty was not exempt. The righteous king was one who "has pity on the weak and the needy" (Ps. 72:13).

Compassion was an integral part of Micah's understanding of righteousness (see Mic. 6:8). "Doing justice" was demonstrated by acts of compassion. "Loving kindness" was demonstrated by acts of compassion. "Walking humbly with God" was demonstrated by acts of compassion.

The Gospels and Compassion

The Gospel writers use the word *compassion* only twelve times. All the references are to Jesus, except in three parables. In the parable of the Wicked Servant, compassion denotes the pity felt by the lord of the slave (Matt. 18:23–25). In the parable of the Prodigal Son, compassion is shown by the father (Luke 15:20). Finally, in the parable of the Good Samaritan, pity is shown by the Samaritan (Luke 10:33).

Although the first two parables are illustrations of God's mercy, the third is clearly a strong statement by Jesus of the way his followers ought to behave: "Go and do likewise" (Luke 10:37). He is urging them to practice the same kind of compassion described in the Old Testament through consideration for others expressed in acts of aid and relief. Jesus also indicates a communal obligation by hinting at the compassion and mercy that one member of the covenant community owes to another. The implication is clear: as God loves us, we are to love one another and to be compassionate (merciful) as God is compassionate.

It is in Jesus' acts that we see most clearly what compassion meant to him. His mercy and pity were shown not only in teachings such as the Beatitudes but in his acts of healing. The Gospels portray him as one who fulfilled the words of Isaiah 53:4: "Surely he has borne our infirmities and carried our diseases." He is the Messiah whose compassion leads him to restore suffering people to health and well-being. The Gospels focus particularly on his compassion toward those who were outcasts or marginal in his day: lepers, women, demoniacs, tax collectors, sinners, children, and Gentiles. These acts of compassion toward "outsiders" defied the Jewish expectation that the Messiah's ministry would be among pious Jews alone. Jesus' inaugural sermon in the synagogue of Nazareth declared his intention to "bring good news to the poor, proclaim release to the captives and recovery of sight to the blind, to let the oppressed go free" (see Luke 14:16–21). The congregation was impressed at these compassionate words until Jesus suggested that God's compassion is extended toward Gentiles as well as Jews. Then their limited understanding of compassion was so outraged that they attempted to throw him over a cliff.

One undeniable mark of Jesus' compassion is the way he showed total acceptance of people who were considered unacceptable. He was even willing to defy tradition and custom by actually touching those considered ritually "unclean." Men, especially rabbis, were forbidden to touch women who might be having their monthly uncleanness. Such an act would make a man unclean, and he would have to undergo the tediousness of ritual purification at the Temple (Lev. 15:19). Nevertheless, Jesus touched the hand of Peter's mother-in-law (Matt. 8:14); he did not reprove the woman who "defiled" him by touching the fringe of his cloak (Matt. 9:20); he took Jairus's daughter by the hand (Matt. 9:25); and he allowed a "sinful woman" to bathe his feet with her tears and dry them with her hair (Luke 7:38).

Jesus also defied Old Testament prohibitions recorded in Numbers 5 and 19 about touching lepers (Matt. 8:3) and the dead (Luke 7:14). In all these cases, he placed compassion above ritual observances. New Testament scholar Lamar Williamson comments, "Jesus' divine authority is placed at the service of desperately importunate people. His sensitivity can make us patient, just as his powerful care, working through our faith, can make us whole."[4]

One of Jesus' clearest statements about the importance of compassion is in the twenty-fifth chapter of Matthew, in which he claims that service to the poor is actually a requirement of his kingdom. In this chapter, he rejects the common understanding that eternal life is gained by scrupulous observance of the rules of piety. Instead, he claims that we experience eternal life in our acts of compassion for the hungry and thirsty, the naked, the sick, and those in prison. As God has acted toward us, fulfilling the covenant relationship with love, mercy, and compassion, so we must act in love toward others, fulfilling the demands laid on us by the covenant.

A highly respected model of this kind of compassion is Mother Teresa. She expressed her concern for the poor in vivid language:

> If sometimes our poor people have had to die of starvation, it is not because God didn't care for them, but because you and I didn't give, were not instruments of love in the hands of God, to give them that bread, to give them that clothing; because we did not recognize him, when once more Christ came in distressing disguise—in the hungry woman, in the lonely man, in the homeless child, and seeking for shelter.[5]

Chapter 8

Discipleship

The teachings of Jesus antagonize religious and political authorities, who eventually oversee his execution on a cross. On the third day, however, by the power of God's Spirit, Jesus is raised from the dead. Prior to returning to the Father, he commands his followers to go throughout the world proclaiming his resurrection and preaching his message of compassion. Jesus instructs his followers to model their behavior on his own words and deeds. He tells them to teach other people to do the same, so that both his original followers and others from all nations will together be his disciples. As disciples, their lives are to be characterized first and foremost by service to all people.

In some ways, the concept of discipleship wraps up our whole series of studies on biblical themes. Remember the path we have traversed through the Scriptures. According to the Bible, we have been *created* in the image of God and have become part of a *covenantal* community, called the *people of God*. We have also been called to live a life of *righteousness*. In spite of our *failures*, we continue to be given *hope* for this life and for eternity through the *compassionate love* of Christ. Our lives as God's people in this world, therefore, are now to be defined by Christ's own life.

Discipleship is a large concept. Its ramifications for our lives are, perhaps, greater than we sometimes wish to admit. After all, the word itself implies that we are following someone else. In a culture that glorifies leadership, this is not necessarily easy to accept. Notice all the books written on the topic of being a leader, while the number of works detailing how to be an excellent *follower* stands somewhere between few and none. Although the very topic of discipleship may go against the grain in our society, discipleship is nonetheless an extremely important element for any serious follower of Jesus.

The Presupposition of Discipleship

The theme of discipleship assumes a connection to Jesus Christ, but what is that connection? To get at this question, let's think about a few verses from Paul's letter to the Romans:

> But you are not in the flesh; you are in the Spirit, since the Spirit of God dwells in you. Anyone who does not have the Spirit of Christ does not belong to him. But if Christ is in you, though the body is dead because of sin, the Spirit is life because of righteousness. If the Spirit of him who raised Jesus from the dead dwells in you, he who raised Christ from the dead will give life to your mortal bodies also through his Spirit that dwells in you.
>
> (Rom. 8:9–11)

The deepest connection between Jesus and the disciples—and us!—surfaces in the conception of "union with Christ." Notice how this passage in Romans calls us "children of God" or "heirs of God," that is, people who belong to the divine family. Incredibly, Paul can say that "Christ is in you (or us)." The other way he expresses this is to say, "The Spirit is in you (or us)."

If you think back to the Temple in the Old Testament, you can get a sense for what this means. God's presence was to be found in the Temple. This does not imply that God was limited to that holy space. Neither does it suggest that God was there literally, in a physical sense. Rather God had made that place a point of contact for God's people. The Lord's presence in the Temple meant that Israel's relationship with God was firm, immediate, assured, and vital. Now, in this new era after Jesus Christ's coming to earth, the divine presence, in the person of Jesus Christ, inhabits us—both as a people gathered together in the church and as individual believers. Christ's life is just as real in us as was God's presence in the Temple in Jerusalem. This is called the "indwelling of Christ" or the "indwelling of the Spirit."

In the early second century, Ignatius, the bishop of the church of Antioch, was transported to Rome to be executed for his Christian faith. On the way, he wrote letters, or epistles, to congregations in Asia Minor. The letters are similar to those written by Paul some sixty years earlier. Ignatius identifies himself in each letter as "Ignatius, the God-bearer."[1] At times, he speaks of his hearers also as "God-bearers." At other times he calls them "Christ-bearers" or "Spirit-bearers." In other words, Ignatius is suggesting that, in an important sense, disciples of Jesus carry Christ—or God, or the Spirit—within them in their daily lives, as he himself was bearing Christ across the eastern Mediterranean basin toward Rome.

Think of what this might mean for us. Imagine if we were consciously to keep in mind this phenomenal thought: *We, too, carry Christ along in our everyday lives*. Would this thought change some of our behaviors? Would it have some effect on the thoughts we think, the words we say, or the deeds we do? It should, because it is the basis for our discipleship, our attempts to live lives that are determined and defined by Jesus Christ.

Now notice that the apostle Paul is not suggesting that we will do any of this perfectly. Verse 10 refers to our bodies being "dead because of sin." The final word, though, is that our spirits are alive "because of righteousness." Discipleship is a progressive thing. Gradually, over a lifetime, we should be making strides toward being conformed into Christ's image as better disciples.

What sorts of things will a life of discipleship display? Or, more accurately, what sorts of things will gradually be developing along the way on our earthly walk with Christ? We could talk about many things here, but in this chapter we concentrate on three in particular.

A Learning Spirit

The root meaning of *disciple* is simply "learner" or "pupil." Curiously, the Greek word is *mathetes*, and it has provided the root for our English word, *mathematics*. If you recall how much discipline math requires, you may not find this so curious after all. In the Gospels, "discipleship" is used primarily of the twelve followers who were especially connected to Jesus. Luke, for example, describes the calling of the Twelve in this way:

> Now during those days he went out to the mountain to pray; and he spent the night in prayer to God. And when day came, he called his disciples and chose twelve of them, whom he also named apostles.
>
> (Luke 6:12–13)

Nevertheless, the word is never restricted to those twelve men; both in the Gospels and in the book of Acts, it implies a broader reference to all people who believe in Jesus. In Matthew, where *disciple* is a particularly beloved word, the Twelve—in both their successes and failures—appear to be models for all persons who desire to follow the Lord. Thus, in the famous Great Commission at the end of the Gospel, Jesus instructs the disciples, now minus Judas, "Go therefore and make disciples of all nations" (Matt. 28:19). It is clear that, for Matthew, those who have been baptized in Jesus' name and are learning to live according to his teachings deserve to be called disciples.

The awareness that discipleship involves learning goes far back into the Old Testament. Remember the Shema in Deuteronomy, the words that frame the Jewish faith up to the present. After intoning the solemn declaration "Hear, O

Israel: The LORD is our God, the LORD alone," Deuteronomy instructs the people, "Keep these words that I am commanding you today in your heart. Recite them to your children and talk about them when you are at home and when you are away, when you lie down and when you rise" (Deut. 6:4–7).

The implication here is that Israel should be continually learning more fully God's will for the people. The book of Proverbs, especially, promotes this theme. As we saw in our discussion of creation, this book promulgates practical wisdom. The writer, speaking in the name of Wisdom, admonishes children—and us readers as well—to learn the commands and teachings that will keep us on the right path through life:

> Listen, children, to a father's instruction,
>   and be attentive, that you may gain insight;
> for I give you good precepts:
>   do not forsake my teaching.
>   (Prov. 4:1–2)

A little later in the book, we hear an even more pointed appeal:

> To you, O people, I call,
>   and my cry is to all that live.
> O simple ones, learn prudence;
>   acquire intelligence, you who lack it.
> Hear, for I will speak noble things,
>   and from my lips will come what is right.
>   (8:4–6)

It is not difficult to recognize the influence this sort of admonition had on the early church. Jesus' own words, as they are presented in Matthew, imply that his teachings are as authoritative as those of the Old Testament Torah.

You might think of the series of contrasts in the Sermon on the Mount in Matthew 5:21–48. Notice how Jesus begins with the words "You have heard that it was said . . ." Then comes the contrast: "But I say to you . . ." The effect is startling: this man Jesus claims the right to make emendations to the divine Law of Israel. No wonder Matthew concludes the Sermon on the Mount with a comment that the crowds were astounded, "for [Jesus] taught them as one having authority, and not as their scribes" (Matt. 7:29).

Not only did Jesus teach, however, he also acted out the messages that he taught. Jesus becomes, as Dale Allison puts it, "the great illustrator of his injunctions."[2] The result is that followers of Jesus are expected to learn from both his words and his deeds. This carries the image of listening and learning a long step beyond what we saw with Proverbs. There, Wisdom "cries out in the street" (Prov. 1:20), calling us to "hear instruction and be wise" (8:33) and promising, "Happy is the one who listens to me" (8:34). The book of Proverbs promotes the virtue of following the words of a personified Wisdom.

In the Gospels, and particularly in Matthew, Wisdom has taken human form. Early in the first Gospel, we read about this One who goes up to a mountain— the traditional place of divine revelation—and teaches deep mysteries and radiant wisdom. The first teachings are what we have come to call the Beatitudes: "Blessed are the poor in spirit"; "Blessed are the meek"; and "Blessed are the merciful" (see Matt. 5:3–11). Wisdom, personified before, has now taken on human form. It is not for nothing that the New Testament can say it flat out: Jesus is the "Word of God" (Rev. 19:13). Jesus is "the power of God and the *wisdom* of God" (1 Cor. 1:24, italics added). Jesus is all that Wisdom literature had said and more, for he is Wisdom itself, come in human flesh. Thus, his disciples— both then and now—are to listen to and learn from Jesus' words and his deeds.

This readiness to learn, this willingness to be taught, is a prime mark of discipleship. It implies two very specific things for our practice of faith. In the first place, it involves an intense engagement with the words and deeds of Jesus (and the rest of the Scriptures, as well). Reading occasionally will not suffice. Regular, concentrated study is required. This is not always easy for us. In a culture of "quick reads" and throwaway books, the very idea of returning again and again to the Scriptures may seem foreign. Likewise, in a time when we seek the latest, newest information and research, relying on something so ancient may seem counterproductive. Yet the Scriptures, as many of the saints have said, reveal their greatest depths only when our reading is frequent, intensive, and long-term.

In the second place, listening and learning require a continuing commitment to growing in faith and discipleship. In *A Teachable Spirit*, a book about the teaching ministry in the church, Richard Osmer refers to the lifelong nature of learning:

> A teachable spirit is not to be confined to the first stages of the Christian life, however. It is not merely a part of the excitement and zeal that many newly converted Christians feel. Rather, it is an attitude that characterizes piety throughout the Christian life. As Christians develop in faith, they become *more* teachable, not less.[3]

There is an obvious implication for us in this comment. As we have moved along in our Christian lives, have we become more teachable? If asked, would others affirm that we possess a "teachable spirit"?

It should be clear that discipleship, which has the sense of "learner" at its root, will be possible for us only if we seek to cultivate a spirit of learning. By the same token, it is possible to cultivate such a spirit only if we also possess an attitude of humility. This opens up a new field for discussion, however, and so we look at this topic separately.

A Humble Spirit

There is an old cartoon that shows some monks meditating on a mountain. One glances at the other with a peeved look in his eyes and says, "What do you mean *you* taught *me* humility?" Humility seems to be very hard for us human beings to practice continuously and consistently. In the popular production *Godspell*, the primary action revolves around recitation of words of Jesus from the Gospels. If you watch the play looking for it, you will notice that many of Jesus' words either explicitly or implicitly urge his hearers to be humble. Just think of these quotes from the play: "Love your neighbor as yourself." "Do not call anyone rabbi or master." "Whoever would be great among you must be your servant."

Why is it that humility seems to come so hard for us? Perhaps some of that is due to the mixed messages that we hear about humility in the culture at large. Not just sports teams but also auto rental companies, rival banks, colleges, and even school districts love to cry out, "We're number one." In sports there is a caveat of sorts: the winner is expected to say nice things about the loser. The winner is supposed to appear humble—in victory. Thus, on the one hand, we are told to be humble, but on the other, the message is "Be the best that you can be. Stand up for yourself. Be assertive. Take pride in your accomplishments. Play by the rules, but win!"

For many of us, the result is that we seem to swing, pendulum-like, back and forth between pride and insecurity. To counter feelings of low self-esteem and doubt, we assert ourselves. In order not to appear prideful when we have done something well, we put on an air of exaggerated humility. So, in a manner similar to the ancient wisdom, we seek a middle way—we try to act in a way that is neither too prideful nor too humble. We seek to display just the right amount of assertiveness for the specific situation in which we find ourselves. This is good advice, but we may fall into a trap here, focusing primarily on how we appear to others. Are we humble enough? Assertive enough? The more important issue, however, is deeper: Are we indeed humble people?

From Paul's words in 1 Corinthians, it is clear that humility was a problem for many of the people in that congregation. The Corinthian Christians seemed to boast about everything they could think of. They called attention to their possession of marvelous spiritual gifts, to their abilities to speak eloquently, to their freedom to eat meat offered to idols, and to their pride in which person had baptized them. To all of that Paul responds, "Let the one who boasts, boast in the Lord" (1 Cor. 1:31). Paul's words are a paraphrase of words of the prophet Jeremiah:

> Thus says the LORD: Do not let the wise boast in their wisdom, do not let the mighty boast in their might, do not let the wealthy boast in their wealth; but let those who boast boast in this, that they understand and know me, that I am the LORD; I act with steadfast love, justice, and righteousness in the earth, for in these things I delight, says the LORD.
>
> (Jer. 9:23–24)

Notice the subtle point that Jeremiah makes. He calls those who hear his words (and we who read them) not to boast in their own particular special blessings. We should not boast in our own wisdom, might, or wealth, for example. Rather, any "boasting" should concentrate on the fact that we "understand and know God." In other words, we can focus on ourselves, or we can look away from ourselves to the infinitely greater One, God. That is straightforward enough. The more subtle point is the implication of knowing God. The prophet characterizes this God as the One who acts with "love, justice, and righteousness." And so should we.

Paul points the Corinthians in the same direction. If we wish to follow Jesus Christ and practice discipleship, we must wrap ourselves in the garments of humility. After all, as the eternal Word, Jesus Christ had the whole universe as his footstool, but he came down to live in this world and, indeed, to be killed in humiliation on a cross. That's why the apostle Paul—who would appear to have had some knowledge of, and problems with, pride himself—writes that he "decided to know nothing among [the Corinthians] except *Jesus Christ, and him crucified*" (1 Cor. 2:2, italics added).

This was not a popular message then, and it isn't now. The uniqueness of the message is exactly this claim: faith in Christ presents a God who dies on a cross. It offers a God who, as Lord of all creation, is humble. As Paul tells us, this message was foolishness to the Greeks. It has continued to be that for many folks from that day to this, because it goes against the grain of our longings for self-protection, self-gain, and status in the eyes of our family, our friends, and our community.

Being humble is really simply having a correct view of ourselves and of our place in this world. Think for a moment of the theme we discussed in the first chapter, *creation*. Each of us has been created in "the image of God." We have value and we can have a sense of worth because we have a connection to God. The act of creation also suggests two reasons that we should be humble. First, we are not God. We are only, as glorious as that is, creatures made in the image of God. We have our place in the grand scheme of the universe, but it is not the highest place. Second, each human being, including every man, woman, and child—every African, Asian, European, Latino—is created in God's image. Thus we all exist on an equal plane.

There is a wonderful line in a little-known novel by Milton Steinberg titled *As a Driven Leaf.* The story is set in the years after the destruction of Jerusalem. The main character, Elisha, is a learned rabbi. While still a boy, his own father passes away, and Elisha is brought up by a stern but caring uncle, Amram. At a certain point, Elisha rushes home after receiving word that Amram is on his deathbed. He arrives in time to hear Amram's final words: "I am content. I have set you firmly in the ways of our people. Now may He take my soul for I am not better than my fathers."[4]

"For I am not better than my fathers." The matter-of-fact tone in which Amram pronounces these words is worth pondering. Perhaps the hardest thing about discipleship is humility. Every now and then, it is probably worth examining our attitudes and actions. If you decide to do so, you might ask yourself questions like these: "Would others call me a 'humble person'?" "What can I do to develop a more humble attitude?" "How can I act in ways that will reflect a more humble spirit?"

A Serving Spirit

When you read the New Testament, one of the words you encounter frequently is *servant.* Occasionally, the word translates *diakonos,* from which we get "deacon." The more significant Greek word, however, is *doulos,* which is translated both "servant" and "slave." It is a strong word, and it suggests a level of ownership that does not come out entirely in the English word *servant.* The apostle Paul uses the word to underline the fact that he—and we—belong to Christ. As he writes to the Corinthian Christians, "You are not your own . . . you were bought with a price" (1 Cor. 6:19–20).

This sense of ownership, of servanthood, goes far back in biblical history. That Israel is to serve God by obeying the divine law is implied already in the first of the Ten Commandments. God declares, "I am the LORD your God, who brought you out of the land of Egypt, out of the house of slavery; you shall have no other gods before me" (Exod. 20:2–3). No longer do the Israelites serve the Egyptians; now they serve God. Later, when Joshua has brought the people into the land of Palestine, there is a wonderful scene in which, near the end of his life, he challenges the people to remain faithful to the Lord: "Now if you are unwilling to serve the LORD, choose this day whom you will serve, . . . but as for me and my household, we will serve the LORD" (Josh. 24:15).

With a solemn oath, the people promise to obey God: "Far be it from us that we should forsake the LORD to serve other gods . . . we also will serve the LORD, for he is our God" (vv. 16, 18).

Interestingly, the title "servant of the Lord" appears regularly in the Old Testament with an undercurrent of approval. The books of Moses already speak of Abraham (Gen. 26:24) and Moses (Exod. 14:31) in tones of honor: they are "my servants." Likewise, prophets such as Isaiah, Jeremiah, and Ezekiel portray the people as a whole as cherished servants of the Lord. For example, even in the midst of strong words of judgment, Jeremiah writes, "Have no fear, my servant Jacob, says the LORD, and do not be dismayed, O Israel" (Jer. 30:10). The requirement to serve God involves great responsibility and serious accountability, as we saw already in chapter 3, but it also carries a great privilege: to be cared for by a loving and compassionate God.

In the New Testament, followers of Jesus are regularly likened to servants or slaves. Jesus reminds his disciples that a "servant is not above his master" (Matt. 10:24, RSV). He cautions them to liken themselves to slaves who do not expect thanks for the work they have been ordered to do: "So you also, when you have done all that you were ordered to do, say, 'We are worthless slaves; we have done only what we ought to have done!'" (Luke 17:10). Not infrequently, Jesus tells parables that reflect the situations of slaves as examples for his hearers. You might think of the parable of the Faithful and Unfaithful Servants (Matt. 24:45–51) and the parable of the Talents (25:14–30). In the latter parable, the master addresses the good servants, who have made good investments with the moneys they received, with the words "Well done, good and trustworthy slave" (Matt. 25:21, 23). The servant who hid his talent, in contrast, hears this condemnation: "You wicked and lazy slave!" (v. 26).

Jesus' own life carried a continual undertone of service. The great hymn to Christ's humility and exaltation in Philippians 2 puts it in these words: "though he was in the form of God, [he] did not regard equality with God as something to be exploited, but emptied himself, taking the form of a slave" (Phil. 2:6–7). Jesus came, in other words, to serve, and that service takes him, according to this biblical hymn, all the way to "death on a cross" (v. 8).

Apart from the crucifixion itself, the most telling illustration Jesus gives us of serving others is found in the familiar story of the footwashing in John 13. As you may remember, at Jesus' Last Supper with his disciples, he pours water into a bowl and begins to wash the disciples' feet. At the end of this surprising scene, Jesus tells them he is providing an example for them to follow. The way he has acted is the way they ought to treat one another.

The footwashing shows service so well because it completely reverses normal procedure. In first-century Palestine, children washed their parents' feet, wives could wash their husbands' feet, and servants regularly performed the same service for their masters and for visitors to the household. For a teacher to wash his disciples' feet was simply unheard of. Quite naturally, therefore, Peter protests the action. Jesus replies in a way that makes his intentions crystal clear: "You call me Teacher and Lord—and you are right, for that is what I am. So if I, your Lord and Teacher, have washed your feet, you also ought to wash one another's feet" (John 13:13–14).

Jesus closes with the comment "If you know these things, blessed are you if you do them" (John 13:17). Knowing and doing are two different things. We realize this well enough, but we don't always care to admit it. It is one thing to talk in glowing terms of the virtues of serving others. It may be another thing to think about the practical implications of such service. Nor was it easy for the disciples. These same twelve had discussed—we can assume more than once—which of them would be the "greatest" in the kingdom (Mark 9:34). It was stunning to realize that Jesus truly wished them to display the attitude of one who washes another's feet.

How might we apply this stunning realization to ourselves? Where can we best serve Jesus in our own lives? What does our discipleship look like, and what should it look like? It is easy to point to the outstanding cases of persons such as Mother Teresa or Saint Francis or Father Damian. Their sense of service led them to change lifestyles and cultures in order to do the work to which God was calling them. Many others whose names are not familiar to us have embraced similar vocations, as they have gone into inner cities, traveled to faraway countries, and entered dangerous settings in service of Christ.

Most of us will probably not hear such calls. Rather, we will hear much more mundane calls to service. We will be called to volunteer in a soup kitchen, or to care for a parent in the advanced stages of Alzheimer's, or to help an adult to gain basic literacy skills. We will be called to volunteer in a local school, or to take meals to shut-ins, or to serve in the volunteer fire department. We will be called to be faithful spouses, dedicated parents, caring neighbors, and honest colleagues. The ways we will be called to serve are as varied as are our lives, our gifts, and our situations.

The only unchanging element is the desire to be a disciple of Jesus Christ and to serve him faithfully. It is what Paul meant when he wrote to the Galatians, encouraging them that they should "through love become slaves to one another" (Gal. 5:13). As hard as that sometimes is, it remains a pearl of great price, because it links us in the chain of all those people down through history who have tried to be humble disciples of the Lord, have sought to serve him, and have heard these words at the end of their earthly course: "Well done, good and faithful servant. Enter into the joy of your master" (Matt. 25:21, RSV).

Lesson Plans

Lesson Plan for Chapter 1: Creation

Advance preparation:

- Make copies of the words from Psalm 8:1–5, 9 for the opening.
- Get a copy of Johnson's *God's Trombones*, and practice reading the sermon on Genesis until you are comfortable with it.
- Prepare the chart on the Days of Creation in Genesis 1 in advance, so that you will be ready to fill it in with the group at the appropriate time. (If you know in advance who will be in the class, you can ask the members to read chapter one in the study book and to do this exercise as an assignment before the class meets.)
- Search a number of magazines to collect a variety of pictures that depict the created world.
- Procure crayons, pencils, and colored pens, along with drawing paper.

1. Welcome and Opening Prayer (5 minutes)

Welcome people to the class and do any "housekeeping" details that may be necessary. Let them introduce themselves if they do not know one another. Read these verses from Psalm 8, either in unison or responsively:

> O LORD, our Sovereign,
>   how majestic is your name in all the earth!
> You have set your glory above the heavens.
>   Out of the mouths of babes and infants
> you have founded a bulwark because of your foes,
>   to silence the enemy and the avenger.
> When I look at your heavens, the work of your fingers,
>   the moon and the stars that you have established;
> what are human beings that you are mindful of them,
>   mortals that you care for them?
> Yet you have made them a little lower than God,
>   and crowned them with glory and honor. . . .

O Lᴏʀᴅ, our Sovereign,
how majestic is your name in all the earth!

2. Group Sharing: Thoughts of Creation (10 minutes)

A. Ask members of the class to reflect on their images and ideas of creation.
How do they picture the thoughts in God's mind or the feelings in God's
heart in the process of creating the universe and this earth? Allow a few
moments for reflection and then invite people to share their ideas and
images.

B. Read aloud James Weldon Johnson's sermon on Genesis in *God's Trombones*. Ask people to close their eyes while they listen to the story. Ask
them to be aware of the images that strike them most strongly. Share these
as a group.

3. Bible Research (25 minutes)

A. Encountering the Text of Genesis 1 (10 minutes)

  • Place the diagram (p. 79) on a chalkboard or easel. Then ask the group
    to fill in the blanks with the key creations on each of the days.

  • Ask the class to point out the similarities in structure in the events of cre-
    ation. They should be able to observe parallels both vertically (between
    the movement from day 1 to day 3 and from day 4 to day 6) and hori-
    zontally (between day 1 and day 4, day 2 and day 5, etc.). Then encour-
    age them to expand on the comments in the study book regarding the
    implications of these similarities for our understanding of the creation.

B. The Beauty and Awesomeness of Creation (15 minutes)

  • Ask the class to consider the quotation from John Calvin in this chapter.
    Would the writer of Psalm 104 have agreed with Calvin? How might the
    writer and Calvin be "saying the same thing differently"? Then ask class
    members whether they recall similar experiences in their own lives. What
    is it about certain kinds of things that seems to draw our thoughts to God
    or to the beauty of creation?

  • Pass out pictures you have collected that show images of the created
    world. You might find them in *National Geographic, Newsweek,* or other
    publications. Try to have a wide variety available. Pictures of a forest,
    lake, or mountains are just some examples. DNA structure, human faces,
    and colorful galaxies are others. If possible, let people choose a picture
    they are attracted to. Then request that they share their reaction, asking:
    "What does this say about creation to you?"

4. Creative Expression: The Enjoyment of Creation (15 minutes)

A. The major focus of this chapter is rejoicing in God's creation and enjoying its beauty and mystery. Ask the class to concentrate on the ideas of

Day 1	Day 4
Day 2	Day 5
Day 3	Day 6

"enjoying" and "rejoicing in." What do these terms mean to them? How are they similar and different?

B. Now ask the class to choose one or two things that they find to be beautiful in this world. Ask them to meditate on them briefly: What is it about them that they find to be lovely, mysterious, and attractive?

C. Have crayons, pencils, and colored pens available, along with various colors of paper. Ask the class to try (regardless of whether they are good at art) to depict something of this beauty on paper. Instruct them to try to sense enjoyment and rejoicing in God, perhaps in an attitude of prayer, as they create their image.

5. Closing (5 minutes)

Ask people to return to the sheet from Psalm 8, used at the beginning of the lesson. Let them reflect on it silently for a few moments, then read it together once again as a closing prayer.

※※※※※※

Assignment for Chapter 2:

- Read chapter 2 in the study book.
- Read Genesis 12:1–10. What is God promising?
- Read Exodus 19:3–6. Again, what is God promising?
- Take a few minutes to make a list of covenant promises you have made.

Lesson Plan for Chapter 2: Covenant

Advance preparation:

- Make copies of Psalm 119:132–135 for the opening unison reading.
- Be sure newsprint and markers are on hand.
- Make a copy for each participant of the sheet title "My Covenant with God" (see step 5).

1. Opening Prayer (5 minutes)

Read Psalm 119:132–135 in unison:

> Turn to me and be gracious to me,
>   as is your custom toward those who love your name.
> Keep my steps steady according to your promise,
>   and never let iniquity have dominion over me.
> Redeem me from human oppression,
>   that I may keep your precepts.
> Make your face shine upon your servant,
>   and teach me your statutes.

2. Brainstorming (10 minutes)

- A. Ask: "What is a covenant?" Write participants' answers on newsprint and post them.
- B. Ask: "What covenant promises did you think of in your homework assignment?" Write these also on newsprint.

3. Bible Research (10 minutes)

Ask half the group to turn to Genesis 15 and half to Genesis 17. Give each group a sheet of newsprint. Ask them to read the texts silently and then write on the newsprint the components of the promise to Abraham. When both groups have finished, ask for a quick oral summary. Are there differences in the promises in these chapters?

4. Question and Answer (20 minutes)

Discuss answers to these questions:
- What does it mean to say the covenant with Abraham is unilateral?
- In what way is it a covenant of trust?
- What does God promise?
- What is expected of Abraham?
- How does the Mosaic covenant differ from the Abrahamic one?
- What is the core of the Mosaic covenant promise?
- Why was the Mosaic covenant important for the people of God?
- Why is obedience to God's laws important for us?

5. Creative Writing (10 minutes)

Give each participant a copy of the sheet titled "My Covenant with God" (p. 83). Ask them to write down three promises they will make.

6. Closing (5 minutes)

Ask for two or three volunteers to share one of the promises they have made. Close with a prayer of commitment.

⌒⌒⌒⌒⌒⌒⌒

Assignment for Chapter 3:
- Read chapter 3 in the study book.
- Read Exodus 19:1–9. What promises does God make to the people of Israel?
- Read Galatians 3:23–29. Who all is included in "Abraham's offspring"?
- Think of what the church looks like in (and to) the world today. How does it match up to what you read in these two passages?

My Covenant with God

God has promised:

    1. To go with me;

    2. To be my friend;

    3. To sustain and comfort me.

I promise to show my trust in these promises by:

1. _____

_____

_____

_____

_____

2. _____

_____

_____

_____

_____

3. _____

_____

_____

_____

_____

Lesson Plan for Chapter 3: The People of God

Advance preparation:

- Make copies of Psalm 133:1–3 for the opening unison reading.
- Be sure newsprint and markers are on hand.
- Bring a pair of shoes or, better, sandals to class.
- Again, bring Johnson's *God's Trombones* to class.
- Write the questions for Galatians 6:1–10 on newsprint (step 3.D), or make individual sheets for class members.

1. Opening Prayer (5 minutes)

Read Psalm 133:1–3 in unison:

> How very good and pleasant it is
>   when kindred live together in unity!
> It is like the precious oil on the head,
>   running down upon the beard,
> on the beard of Aaron,
>   running down over the collar of his robes.
> It is like the dew of Hermon,
>   which falls on the mountains of Zion.
> For there the LORD ordained his blessing,
>   life forevermore.

2. Setting the Stage (15 minutes)

A. The Meaning of "People" (5 minutes)

- Ask what it is that makes a group of human beings a "people." You might stimulate the group's thinking by asking such questions as: "How many individuals are needed?" "What sorts of common characteristics do a people display?" "What does it mean to speak of 'the English people' or 'the American people'"?
- Place the responses on newsprint.

B. God's Almighty Power (5 minutes)

- Refer the group to the comments on the irresistible power of God in choosing Israel.
- Bring a copy to the class of another sermon by James Weldon Johnson, "Let My People Go," which rehearses the events of the exodus. Read brief sections, along with the concluding lines. Ask the class to consider how the sense of God's almighty power in this sermon impacts on them.

C. "People" and Pride (5 minutes)

- Remind the class of the comment in the text "The temptation to hold onto blessings, honors, or privileges lies close at hand for all of us." Invite the group to think about the implications of that statement for Israel's self-consciousness as a chosen people.
- Ask people to name other examples where "group pride" turns into attitudes of superiority and exclusivity. Where do they see that occurring in our own land and local regions, as well as in the church? Reflect with them on the reasons why such attitudes seem to develop in groups, peoples, and nations—both in the time of Israel and in our own day.

3. *Bible Research (35 minutes)*

A. Leviticus 19:9–18 (10 minutes)

- Divide the class into five groups, and assign each group two verses from this passage in Leviticus. (If the group has fewer than ten members, you may wish to assign two verses to each person or simply to discuss the passage as an entire class.)
- Ask people to discuss their verses, examining what is being commanded and what the purpose of the command might be. How would they apply the underlying principles to their own neighborhood and nation?
- Afterward, invite the groups to share in turn their responses and conclusions.

B. Amos 2:6–7 (10 minutes)

- Bring a pair of sandals or shoes to class with you. Ask the class to estimate the approximate dollar value of the shoes or sandals. Then ask, by way of comparison, how they would assess the value of a human being.
- Remind them of Amos' accusation that the poor are being "sold for a pair of shoes." Discuss whether, and where, they find such things happening in our own society and/or the world. You may wish to ask members of the group to look for such incidents in their newspaper in the coming week and to bring those reports with them to the next class.

C. Galatians 3:26–29 (5 minutes)

- Summarize briefly the discussion in the text about these verses. Focus especially on the concept of "communion of saints."

D. Galatians 6:1–10 (10 minutes)

- Ask people to divide into their earlier groups again. Instruct them to read this passage in their group, and then discuss the following questions in light of this passage. (These should be placed on an easel in advance, or you can prepare them on individual sheets of paper, perhaps with space between the questions for people to jot down notes on the discussion.)

  a. What sorts of characteristics should a "communion of saints" demonstrate?

  b. What can you do to strengthen the "communion of saints" in your own congregation?

4. Closing (5 minutes)

Remind the class that Galatians 6 counsels us, "Bear one another's burdens." Keep people in whatever groups you have placed them in, and give instructions similar to the following:

Please share with your group one joy or concern for which you would like prayer. Then take a few moments to pray for one another. When all prayers have been said and the room becomes quiet, we will close as a whole group.

Close by reading as a prayer the first verse of the hymn "In Christ, there is no east or west."

Assignment for Chapter 4:

- Read chapter 4 in the study book.
- Read Judges 2:11–19. List the phrases that describe the sins of the Israelites. What parallels can you think of in today's world?
- Go through your newspaper or news magazines and tear out pictures, stories, and words that are illustrations of sin. Bring these to class.

Lesson Plan for Chapter 4: Sin

Advance preparation:
- Make copies of the words from Psalm 51:1–2, 10 for the opening.
- Attach to the wall several sheets of newsprint for the "Graffiti Wall." Provide tape and markers.
- Make copies of the questions for the question-and-answer exercise.
- Provide slips of paper for the ritual of forgiveness. Have on hand a metal dish, matches, and a candle.
- Provide copies of the litany of dedication.

1. Opening Prayer (5 minutes)

Read Psalm 51:1–2, 10 in unison:

> Have mercy on me, O God,
>   according to your steadfast love;
> according to your abundant mercy
>   blot out my transgressions.
> Wash me thoroughly from my iniquity,
>   and cleanse me from my sin. . . .
> Create in me a clean heart, O God,
>   and put a new and right spirit within me. Amen.

2. Graffiti Wall (10 minutes)

As participants enter, ask them to attach to the Graffiti Wall any pictures (or other items) they have brought as an illustration of sin. They may use markers to label their contributions. When all have finished, ask what the collection suggests about the meaning of sin.

3. Small Group Discussion: Definitions of Sin (15 minutes)

If the group is large enough, divide into three smaller groups and assign one of the definitions at the beginning of the chapter to each group. Ask them to discuss the comment, decide what important thing it says about sin, and provide a specific example of the kind of sin it describes. Ask each group to select a spokesperson to report their findings. Call the groups back together for brief reports. If your group is small, do this exercise with the group as a whole.

4. Question and Answer (15 minutes)

Give each participant the following questions. Ask them to use the study book to find the answers. After ten minutes, review the answers aloud.

- What are the three major categories of sin in the Old Testament?
- What is original sin?
- What four words describe the cycle of sin in Judges?
- What did the great prophets say about sin during the monarchical period?
- What word describes our role in resolving sin and what word describes God's role?

5. A Ritual of Forgiveness (10 minutes)

Ask participants to write on a slip of paper a sin with which they struggle. Then invite them, one at a time, to bring the paper to the table where a metal dish has been placed and to offer a silent prayer asking God for cleansing and forgiveness. Provide a lighted candle and ask them to burn their slips in the metal dish. If possible, have someone play a hymn such as "Just as I am, without one plea."

6. Closing Benediction (5 minutes)

> "For once you were darkness, but now in the Lord you are light. Live as children of light—for the fruit of the light is found in all that is good and right and true. . . . Peace be to the whole community, and love with faith, from God the Father and the Lord Jesus Christ. Grace be with all who have an undying love for our Lord Jesus Christ." (Ephesians 5:8–9; 6:23–24)

Assignment for Chapter 5:

- Read chapter 5 in the study book.
- Read Proverbs 11 and make notes on what it says about "the righteous."
- Complete the sentence: "To me, righteousness means . . ."

Lesson Plan for Chapter 5: Righteousness

Advance preparation:
- Make copies of the words below from Psalm 85:8–13.
- Have newsprint, tape, and markers on hand.
- Provide paper, pens, and envelopes for letters.
- Provide a pound of potter's clay for each person. This is available at school supply stores.

1. Opening Prayer (5 minutes)

Divide the group into two sections and ask them to read the words from Psalm 85 aloud antiphonally:

Side One: Let me hear what God the Lord will speak,

Side Two: for he will speak peace to his people,

Side One: to his faithful,

Side Two: to those who turn to him in their hearts.

Side One: Surely his salvation is at hand for those who fear him,

Side Two: that his glory may dwell in our land.

Side One: Steadfast love and faithfulness will meet;

Side Two: righteousness and peace will kiss each other.

Side One: Faithfulness will spring up from the ground,

Side Two: and righteousness will look down from the sky.

Side One: The Lord will give what is good,

Side Two: and our land will yield its increase.

Side One: Righteousness will go before him,

Side Two: and will make a path for his steps.

2. Brainstorming (15 minutes)

A. Divide into four small groups. Provide each group with a sheet of newsprint and a marker. Ask them to select one person to record responses. Give each group one of the following words: *righteous, just, justice, justification.* Ask each group to brainstorm what comes to mind with the word they have been given.

B. After ten minutes, ask the groups to bring their newsprint sheets forward and post them on the wall. Quickly review the sheets, noting similarities. Explain that all these words come from the same root in both Hebrew and Greek. Discuss the significance of their interrelation. Ask: What conclusions can we draw about the meaning of righteousness? Has this discussion changed the definition of righteousness you did for homework? In what way?

3. Scripture Research (20 minutes)

A. Briefly review the material in the text describing the three types of righteousness.

B. Divide the class into four groups (not necessarily the same as before). Give each group two of the Scripture references below and ask them to decide which of the three types of righteousness the texts represent (legal, social, religious).

C. When all have finished, have someone from each group read the verses aloud and name the category into which they fall. Some might qualify for more than one category. The verses are:

- Isaiah 9:7
- Isaiah 11:4
- Isaiah 51:1
- Isaiah 61:1–3
- Jeremiah 9:23–24
- Jeremiah 22:3
- Hosea 10:12
- Amos 5:24
- Romans 10:3–4

4. Creative Activities (15 minutes)

- Give participants a choice of the following:
  a. *Letter writing.* Provide paper, pens, and envelopes. Ask the participants to write a letter of appreciation to a person who personifies righteousness, telling what they have learned about righteousness from him or her.
  b. *Sculpting.* Ask participants to use the potter's clay to make a sculpture that represents "righteousness."

- When all have finished, ask the sculptors to display their work on a table in the front of the class. Ask for volunteers from the writers to share a brief word about what they wrote.

5. Closing Challenge (5 minutes)

Read the following:

> When we begin to love our neighbors instead of just talking about love,
>   to worship Christ instead of ourselves,
> then we will begin to understand what righteousness is
>   and to claim it as our own.
> And our response will be like that of the Old Testament people who
>   loved God,
> a response of praise and thanksgiving.

Assignment for Chapter 6:

- Read chapter 6 in the study book.
- Read Lamentations 1. How does it feel to lament deeply?
- Read Lamentations 3:16–33. How does it feel to hope in the face of disappointment?
- List times when you have lamented and hoped. How was your experience similar to or different from that of the writer of Lamentations?

Lesson Plan for Chapter 6: Hope

Advance preparation:

- Make copies of the words below from Psalm 33:18–22.
- Have newsprint, tape, and markers on hand.
- Provide paper and pencils or pens for the writing exercises.
- Have hymnbooks available for the closing if you plan to use the suggested hymn.

1. Opening Prayer (5 minutes)

Read Psalm 33:18–22 in unison:

> Truly the eye of the LORD is on those who fear him,
>   on those who hope in his steadfast love,
> to deliver their soul from death,
>   and to keep them alive in famine.
> Our soul waits for the LORD;
>   he is our help and shield.
> Our heart is glad in him,
>   because we trust in his holy name.
> Let your steadfast love, O LORD, be upon us,
>   even as we hope in you.

2. Setting the Stage: The Latter Years of Judah (10 minutes)

A. Recall for the group the situation in Judah in the last years before the Babylonian exile by reading the story in 2 Kings of the brief reigns of Jehoiachin and Zedekiah. They close out the kingdom, and they are both taken into captivity in Babylon. You may want to read selected verses from the account in chapters 24–25, such as 24:8, 10–14 and 24:17–25:10. Ask the group to imagine the impact of the devastation upon the people of Israel.

B. Remind the group of what they read in Lamentations 1. Ask them to look at the text and point out ways the chapter mirrors the destruction of Jerusalem and the nation.

3. Writing Exercise 1: Lamenting and Grieving (10 minutes)

A. Focus on the personal lament expressed in Lamentations 2. Ask the group whether the grief of the writer seems realistic to them. Can they put themselves in his place? Have they ever experienced a similar sense of grief themselves?

B. Pass out sheets of paper. Ask each person to write one line about the word *grief*. They should not write their names on the papers. Collect the sheets and read them aloud to the group. Then pass the sheets out at random. Ask each person to write a brief lament on the basis of that line. Ask them to hold onto the sheets.

4. Bible Research (30 minutes)

A. Israel's Restoration (10 minutes)

- Give a brief account of how Israel was able to return to the land. Ask the class to compare this stunning political event to amazing changes in foreign affairs in our day. What kinds of similarities do they see in such events and, especially, in the emotions of people who are caught up in the changes?

- The text suggests that "Hope is for those moments when it seems that the fabric of our lives has been ripped and torn beyond repair." Ask class members to share their reflections on this statement. How does it fit with their own understanding of hope? Do they see it as something practical or impractical for the tragedies that can surface in everyday life?

B. An Inheritance in the Heavens (10 minutes)

- Read 1 Peter 1:3–4. Review with the group the connections between hope, the resurrection of Jesus, and our future inheritance. What does hope as an inheritance mean for them? How do they understand it, and how does this thought make them feel?

5. Writing Exercise 2: Hoping (10 minutes)

Tell the group, "We spent some time earlier in this session lamenting. Let's close with some moments for hoping." Request that each person take out the sheet with the lament they wrote. In light of the line about despair, ask them to write a line or two expressing hope in order to offer comfort to the person. (Collect the pages and post them if possible, telling people that they can collect their own sheet at the end of the last class.)

6. Closing (5 minutes)

Sing or read the first stanza of the hymn "Great Is Thy Faithfulness." Alternatively, read Lamentations 3:22–23, 25 as a final prayer of praise to God.

Assignment for Chapter 7:

- Read chapter 7 in the study book.
- Read Psalm 103. What acts show God's compassion?
- Think of an expression of compassion you have received from someone else and be prepared to share it with the group.

Lesson Plan for Chapter 7: Compassion

Advance preparation:

- Make copies of Psalm 145:1–3, 8–10.
- If there is no blackboard, make sure newsprint and markers are on hand.
- Gather an assortment of Sunday school pictures or art reproductions portraying Jesus' acts of ministry.
- Prepare blank bookmarks for each participant.

1. Opening Prayer (5 minutes)

Read Psalm 145:1–3, 8–10 in unison:

> I will extol you, my God and King,
>   and bless your name forever and ever.
> Every day I will bless you,
>   and praise your name forever and ever.
> Great is the LORD, and greatly to be praised;
>   his greatness is unsearchable. . . .
> The LORD is gracious and merciful,
>   slow to anger and abounding in steadfast love.
> The LORD is good to all,
>   and his compassion is over all that he has made.
> All your works shall give thanks to you, O LORD,
>   and all your faithful shall bless you.

2. Word Study (10 minutes)

Instruct the group: "Using the information in the text, discuss the Hebrew and Greek words for compassion (*rachamim* and *splagchna*). What new light have these words shed on the meaning of compassion for you?"

3. Scripture Exploration (20 minutes)

Write the following questions on newsprint or blackboard:

- Why is God called "merciful and gracious"?
- What does this passage teach about God's compassion?

Then divide the class into two groups, and assign each group the following set of Scripture passages. (You may want to write the passages on the newsprint or blackboard as well.) Ask the groups to respond to the questions in light of their assigned passages.

GROUP A:

Isaiah 54:8

Lamentations 3:31–33

Psalm 25:6

Deuteronomy 30:3

Isaiah 14:1

GROUP B:

Jeremiah 42:12

Nehemiah 9:17

Nehemiah 9:19–21

Psalm 111:4

Psalm 145:8–9

When all have finished, write their responses on the newsprint or blackboard.

4. Picture Study (20 minutes)

Gather an assortment of Sunday school pictures or art reproductions portraying Jesus' acts of ministry. Ask participants to choose one of the pictures and describe to the rest of the group what the picture communicates about Jesus' compassion.

5. Closing (5 minutes)

Distribute blank bookmarks and ask participants to write on them one way in which they will demonstrate concrete compassion during the next week. Suggest that they keep the bookmarks in their Bibles until they have accomplished their goal.

Assignment for Chapter 8:

- Read chapter 8 in the study book.
- Read Romans 8:9–17. How are we connected to Jesus, according to Paul?
- How do you understand the concept that "Christ (or the Spirit) is *in* you?" To what degree do you sense this in your life?

Lesson Plan for Chapter 8: Discipleship

Advance preparation:

- Make copies of Psalm 25:4–5, 8–10 for the opening unison reading.
- Be sure newsprint and markers are available.
- Prepare copies of "My Practice of Discipleship" for each participant.

1. Opening Prayer (5 minutes)

Read Psalm 25:4–5, 8–10 in unison:

> Make me to know your ways, O LORD;
>   teach me your paths.
> Lead me in your truth, and teach me,
>   for you are the God of my salvation;
>   for you I wait all day long.
> Good and upright is the LORD;
>   therefore he instructs sinners in the way.
> He leads the humble in what is right,
>   And teaches the humble his way.
> All the paths of the LORD are steadfast love and faithfulness,
>   For those who keep his covenant and his decrees.

2. Brainstorming (5 minutes)

A. Ask: "What is discipleship for you?" Write participants' answers on newsprint.

B. Ask further: "Name things that you think are a part of discipleship." Write these also on newsprint.

3. Bible Research (25 minutes)

A. Read Romans 8:9–17. Ask the class to respond to the following questions:

- How do you understand the concept that "Christ (or the Spirit) is *in* you"?

97

- Name words that describe your feelings about this concept. (List these on newsprint as people name them.)
  B. Divide the class into three groups, if possible. (Groups of two people will also work for this exercise.) Give each group a passage:
  - 1 Corinthians 1:26–2:2 (on humility)
  - Proverbs 4:1–9 (on learning)
  - John 13:3–17 (on serving)

Instruct the groups to read their passage and summarize its basic message as it relates to the topic mentioned. Ask them also to share two or three specific ways they could put what they are discussing into practice. Afterward, ask each group to share their summary and their specific suggestions with the whole class.

4. Group Study Review (10 minutes)

Return to the newsprint list of brainstorming ideas about discipleship done at the beginning of the session.

- Ask: "Do any of these fit under the three (learning, humility, and service) that we have been discussing?"
- Ask further (assuming that additional items will remain on the list): "Which ones are worth a more extended discussion?"
- Ask the group whether they might want to pursue some of these in a continuation of this class.
- Ask also whether the other themes discussed in the past sessions suggest ideas to them for further study as a group. (Make a list of these suggestions for future reference.)

5. Reflective Writing (10 minutes)

Give each participant a copy of the sheet titled "My Practice of Discipleship" (p. 99). Instruct them to write a letter to themselves about how they see those characteristics in themselves, and where they feel they may fall short. After seven or eight minutes, ask them to finish by writing a brief prayer in which they talk to God about their discipleship.

6. Closing (5 minutes)

Ask the group to gather again for prayer. Leave time for all who wish to pray, and then close with the Lord's Prayer.

My Practice of Discipleship

Discipleship means, among other things:

- Having a learning spirit

- Having a humble spirit

- Having a serving spirit

_____

_____

_____

_____

_____

_____

_____

_____

_____

_____

_____

_____

_____

_____

_____

_____

_____

Notes

CHAPTER 1: CREATION

1. James Weldon Johnson, *God's Trombones* (New York: Viking Penguin, 1976), 17.
2. All biblical references are from the New Revised Standard Version unless otherwise noted and are used by permission.
3. Folliott Sandford Pierpoint, "For the Beauty of the Earth," in *The Presbyterian Hymnal* (Louisville, Ky.: Westminster/John Knox Press, 1990), 473.
4. John Calvin, *Institutes of the Christian Religion*, Library of Christian Classics, ed. John T. McNeill, trans. Ford Lewis Battles (Philadelphia: Westminster Press, 1960), 1.5.1.
5. Alan Richardson, *A Theological Word Book of the Bible* (New York: Macmillan, 1953), 283.

CHAPTER 2: COVENANT

1. *Book of Common Worship* (Louisville, Ky.: Westminster/John Knox Press, 1993), 404.
2. Walter Brueggemann, *Genesis*, Interpretation: A Bible Commentary for Teaching and Preaching (Atlanta: John Knox Press, 1982), 37.
3. Bruce Feiler, *Abraham* (New York: William Morrow, 2002), 44.
4. Nancy Byrd Turner, "When Abraham Went out of Ur," in Halford Luccock, *The Questing Spirit* (New York: Coward McCann, 1947), 346.
5. See G. E. Mendenhall, "Covenant," in *The Interpreter's Dictionary of the Bible* (Nashville: Abingdon Press, 1962), 1:719-20.
6. *Sabbath and Festival Prayer Book* (n.p.: The Rabbinical Assembly of America and the United Synagogue of America, 1946), 316.
7. Rachel Henderlite, *A Call to Faith* (Richmond: John Knox Press, 1955), 126-27.
8. Ibid., 136.

CHAPTER 3: THE PEOPLE OF GOD

1. Father Michael Joncas, "On Eagles' Wings," based on the words of Psalm 91, including the reference to wings in verse 4: "He will cover you with his pinions, and under his wings you will find refuge."
2. E. P. Sanders, *Jesus and Judaism* (Philadelphia: Fortress Press, 1985), 218.
3. "In Christ There Is No East or West," by John Oxenham, in *The Presbyterian Hymnal* (Louisville, Ky.: Westminster/John Knox Press, 1990), 439.

CHAPTER 4: SIN

1. John Calvin, *Institutes of the Christian Religion*, Library of Christian Classics, ed. John T. McNeill, trans. Ford Lewis Battles (Philadelphia: Westminster Press, 1960), 2.1.10.

2. Reinhold Niebuhr, *The Nature and Destiny of Man: A Christian Interpretation*, vol. 1: *Human Nature,* The Gifford Lectures (New York: Charles Scribner's Sons, 1964), 16.

3. Walter Brueggemann, *Reverberations of Faith: A Theological Handbook of Old Testament Themes* (Louisville, Ky.: Westminster/John Knox Press, 2002), 195.

4. Ibid., 196.

5. Rachel Henderlite, *A Call to Faith* (Richmond: John Knox Press, 1955), 70.

6. Alan Richardson, *A Theological Word Book of the Bible* (New York: Macmillan, 1953), 228.

7. Frederick Buechner, *Wishful Thinking* (San Francisco: HarperSanFrancisco, 1973), 89.

8. Selected verses from Judges 2:11-19, Today's English Version (New York: American Bible Society, 1976).

9. Alexander MacLaren, *The Books of Deuteronomy, Joshua, Judges, Ruth, and First Book of Samuel* (New York: A. C. Armstrong and Son, 1907), 205.

10. Douglas R. A. Hare, *Matthew*, Interpretation: A Bible Commentary for Teaching and Preaching (Louisville, Ky.: John Knox Press, 1993), 216.

CHAPTER 5: RIGHTEOUSNESS

1. Maimonides, "Eight Degrees of Tsedakah," in *Mishnah Torah* (Gifts to the Needy), 10.

2. *The Guideposts Treasury of Hope* (Carmel, N.Y.: Guideposts Magazine, 1976), 149.

3. Shirley Guthrie, *Christian Doctrine*, rev. ed. (Louisville, Ky.: Westminster John Knox Press, 1994), 314.

4. Ibid., 327.

CHAPTER 6: HOPE

1. For a sobering account of climbing at Mount Everest, see the account of a 1996 expedition in Jon Krakauer, *Into Thin Air* (New York: Anchor Books, 1997).

2. Pat Conroy, *Beach Music* (New York: Bantam Books, 1995), 769.

3. John Calvin, *Institutes of the Christian Religion*, Library of Christian Classics, ed. John T. McNeill, trans. Ford Lewis Battles (Philadelphia: Westminster Press, 1960), 3.25.3.

CHAPTER 7: COMPASSION

1. Phyllis Trible, *God and the Rhetoric of Sexuality*, Overtures to Biblical Theology (Philadelphia: Fortress Press, 1978), 33.

2. Sylvia Nasar, *A Beautiful Mind: The Life of Mathematical Genius and Nobel Laureate John Nash*, A Touchstone Book (New York: Simon & Schuster, 1998), 342.

3. Henri J. M. Nouwen, *With Open Hands* (Notre Dame, Ind.: Ave Maria Press, 1972), 114.

4. Lamar Williamson, *Mark,* Interpretation: A Bible Commentary for Teaching and Preaching (Atlanta: John Knox Press, 1983), 113.

5. Mother Teresa of Calcutta and Brother Roger of Taizé, *Meditations on the Way to the Cross* (New York: Pilgrim Press, 1987), 49.

CHAPTER 8: DISCIPLESHIP

1. See, for example, the greeting in Ignatius's "Epistle to the Ephesians," in *The Apostolic Fathers*, trans. Kirsopp Lake, Loeb Classical Library (Cambridge, Mass.: Harvard University Press, 1975), 1:173.

2. Dale C. Allison Jr., *The Silence of Angels* (Valley Forge, Pa.: Trinity Press International, 1995), 88.

3. Richard Robert Osmer, *A Teachable Spirit: Recovering the Teaching Office in the Church* (Louisville, Ky.: Westminster/John Knox Press, 1990), 53.

4. Milton Steinberg, *As a Driven Leaf* (n.p.: Behrman House, 1939), 79.

For Further Reading

Barton, John. *How the Bible Came to Be*. Louisville, Ky.: Westminster John Knox Press, 1997.

Brown, Robert McAfee. *The Bible Speaks to You*. Louisville, Ky.: Westminster John Knox Press, 1995.

Brueggemann, Walter. *The Bible Makes Sense*. Louisville, Ky.: Westminster John Knox Press, 2001.

———. *Reverberations of Faith: A Theological Handbook of Old Testament Themes*. Louisville, Ky.: Westminster John Knox Press, 2002.

Davis, Kenneth C. *Don't Know Much about the Bible: Everything You Need to Know about the Good Book but Never Learned*. New York: HarperCollins, 1999.

Davison, James E. *The Year of the Bible (Manual* and *Participant's Book)*. Louisville, Ky.: Bridge Resources, 1996.

Guthrie, Shirley. *Christian Doctrine*. Rev. ed. Louisville, Ky.: Westminster John Knox Press, 1994.

Johnson, James Weldon. *God's Trombones*. New York: Viking Penguin, 1976.

Mother Teresa of Calcutta and Brother Roger of Taizé. *Meditations on the Way to the Cross*. New York: Pilgrim Press, 1987.

Nouwen, J. M., Donald P. McNeill, and Douglas A. Morrison. *Compassion: A Reflection on the Christian Life*. New York: Doubleday/Image Books, 1982.